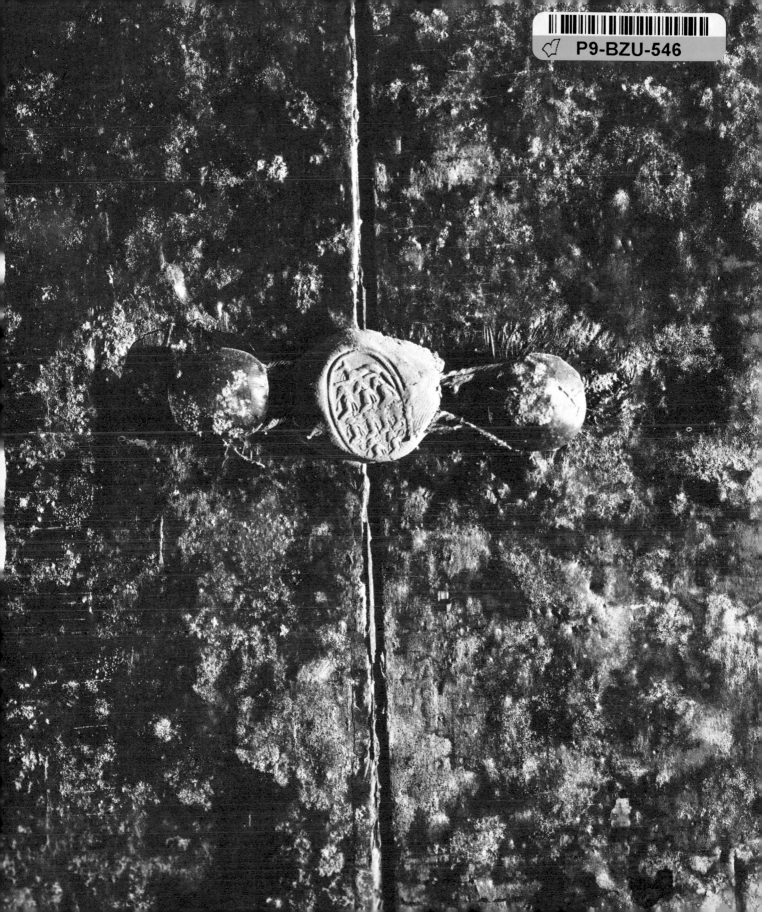

*Well, can you see anything?*

*Yes...*
wonderful things!

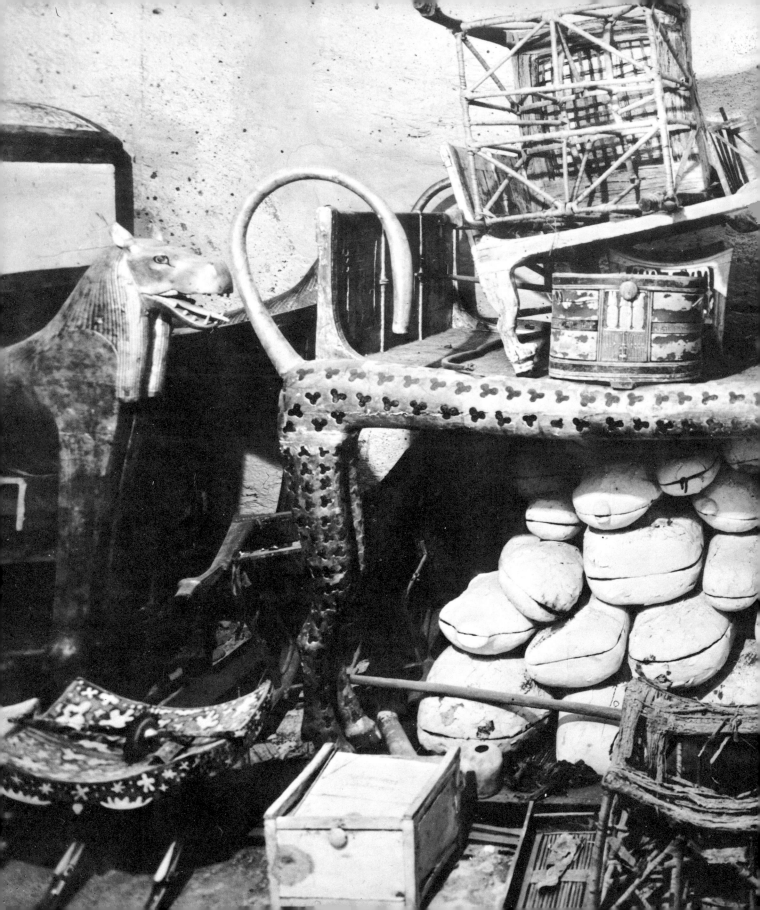

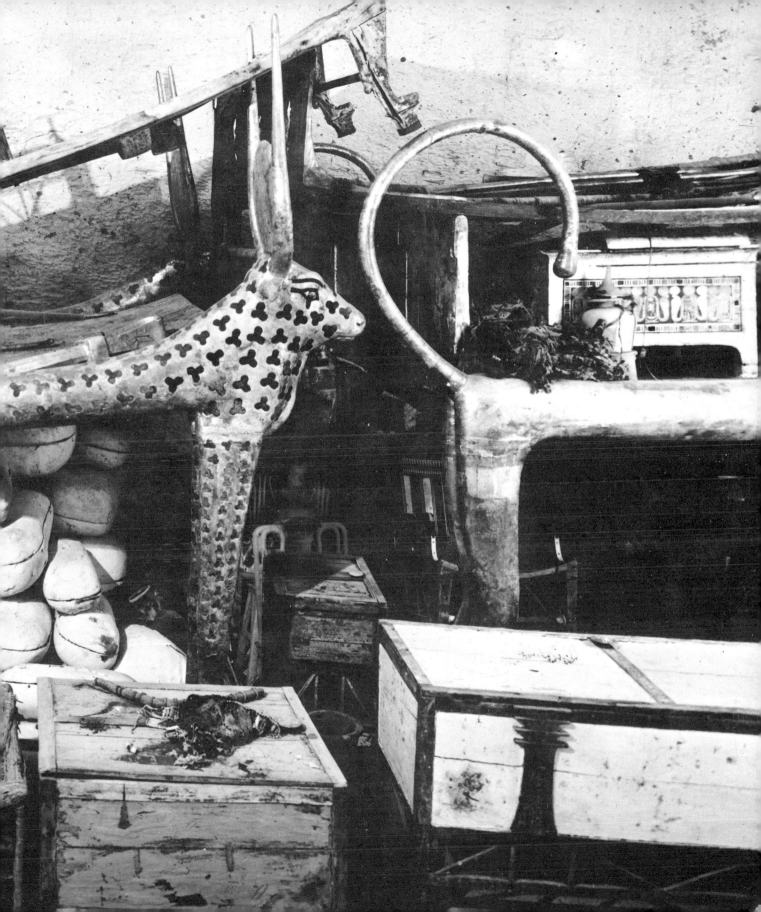

A loan exhibition

from the Department of Antiquities of the Arab Republic of Egypt

to mark the fiftieth anniversary of the discovery of the tomb of Tutankhamun

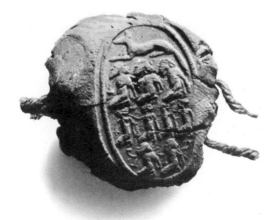

# TREASURES OF TUTANKHAMUN

Sponsored by the Trustees of the British Museum
The Times & the Sunday Times

Held at the British Museum 1972

First published 1972

Text © The Trustees of the British
Museum, *The Times* and the *Sunday Times*
1972
Colour plates © George Rainbird Ltd
1963, 1972 except for number 35
© Thames & Hudson Ltd 1971
All rights reserved

Designed by the Exhibition Office of
the British Museum
Produced by George Rainbird Ltd
Marble Arch House, 44 Edgware Road
London W2

Printed by Westerham Press Ltd
Westerham, Kent
Bound by Cox and Wyman,
Fakenham, Norfolk

ISBN 07 23 0007–00

# FOREWORD

In the year 1922, when the late Earl of Carnarvon and Mr Howard Carter astonished the world by the discovery of the tomb of Tutankhamun and the rich treasure which it contained, no one could have imagined that the fiftieth anniversary of the event would be marked by an exhibition at the British Museum of some of the most important pieces which the two Englishmen, one as patron and the other as archaeologist, had brought to light. That it has happened is a practical expression of the goodwill and friendliness of the Egyptian nation towards this country. It is also a fulfilment of the desire embodied in the Cultural Convention signed in Cairo by the two countries in 1965.

We are deeply conscious not only of the privilege so generously accorded to us by the Government of the Arab Republic of Egypt in granting the loan of the objects in this exhibition, but also of the personal interest in its realization taken by President Anwar es-Sadat, his former Prime Minister, Dr Mahmud Fawzi, and his Deputy Prime Minister and Minister of Information and Culture, Dr Abd el-Qadir Hatim. To all of them we wish to express our gratitude and the gratitude of the thousands of our fellow-countrymen and other visitors who will see the exhibition. Nor must we omit to mention our sense of indebtedness to Dr Sarwat Okasha, Special Adviser to the President on Cultural Affairs, who was Minister of Culture at the time when the plan for holding the exhibition was first conceived. His understanding and warm sympathy with our ambitions greatly encouraged us in our endeavours. Both the present

Ambassador in London of the Arab Republic in Egypt, Mr Kamal ed-Din Rifaat, and his predecessor, Mr Ahmed el-Feki, have given us throughout their most friendly support. Dr Gamal ed-Din Mukhtar and his colleagues in the Department of Antiquities have done everything possible to help us with the practical arrangements.

The Trustees of the British Museum wish to acknowledge the very great assistance which they have received from their partners in the sponsorship of this exhibition, *The Times* and the *Sunday Times*, and particularly from Mr Denis Hamilton, Chairman and Editor-in-Chief, who is also a Trustee of the British Museum. Without their support it would not have been possible to contemplate an exhibition on this scale or to provide the amenities which it offers. They also wish to thank Dr I. E. S. Edwards, Keeper of the Department of Egyptian Antiquities, for all he has done in helping to bring about and to prepare for this exhibition.

Under the terms of the Agreement between the Arab Republic of Egypt and this country, all the proceeds of the exhibition, after deducting expenses, will be paid into the fund sponsored by Unesco for the preservation of the temples of Philae. We greatly hope that the generosity of the Egyptian Government in permitting us to have this exhibition and the efforts of those who have worked to make it a success will be rewarded by a very substantial contribution to this most important project.

TREVELYAN

# THE EXHIBITION

Visitors to this exhibition will perhaps wish to know something about the persons who have been most closely connected with the extensive preparations for its presentation. Reference has already been made to the great assistance which we have received from the officials of the Department of Antiquities of the Arab Republic of Egypt. We are indebted in particular to Dr Gamal ed-Din Mukhtar, Under-Secretary of State to the Ministry of Culture, the late Dr Gamal ed-Din Mehrez, Director of the Department of Antiquities, Dr Henry Riad, Director of the Cairo Museum and his staff, Mme Saniyya Abd el-Al, Keeper of the Tutankhamun Collection, and Dr Zaki Iskandar, Director-General of Technical Affairs. At every stage, from the initial selection of the objects to their departure to London, they gave most liberally of their time and facilitated every operation. Their ready cooperation and quick response to every request for help have earned our deepest gratitude and established ties of friendship which will continue beyond the present exhibition. Professor Ibrahim Shihata visited London as the representative of the Minister of Culture to advise in the drafting of the Agreement between the Government of the Arab Republic of Egypt and the Government of the United Kingdom. In all our negotiations with the Egyptian authorities we have received the greatest assistance from the British Ambassador in Cairo, Sir Richard Beaumont, KCMG, and from members of his staff, especially Mr Alan Urwick, Chargé

d'Affaires when the Agreement was signed, Mr Marrack Goulding, Head of Chancery and Wing-Commander D. R. Barnicoat, Air Attaché. Mr Malcolm Holding and his colleagues both in the Foreign and Commonwealth Office and in the Department of Education and Science have constantly given us their help.

The direction of the exhibition has been in the hands of a committee appointed by the Trustees of the British Museum, whose members were Lord Trevelyan (Chairman), the Earl of Crawford and Balcarres, Mr Denis Hamilton and Professor Misha Black, assisted by the Director of the Museum, Sir John Wolfenden, and the Keeper of Egyptian Antiquities. Two executive committees, under the chairmanship of Mr P. A. Taverner (*The Times* and *Sunday Times*) have been responsible for the detailed planning of the exhibition, and sub-committees have supervised arrangements for security, transport, constructional works and publications. Regular members of these committees, besides Mr Taverner, have been Miss Margaret Hall, Mr J. F. W. Ryde and the Keeper of Egyptian Antiquities (British Museum), Mr B. E. Jeffcott, Mr G. Pearse, Mr M. F. Poole and Mr J. Slatford (*The Times* and *Sunday Times*), Mr P. Saabor and Mr R. Riddell (Thomson Organization), Mr J. Mannings (Security Adviser to the National Museums and Art Galleries), Mr R. Davies and Mr H. F. Rogers (Department of the Environment), Mr George Rainbird and Mrs Joy Law. Miss Margaret Hall and her colleagues in the

Exhibition Office of the Museum have designed both the temporary gallery in which the exhibition will be held and the accommodation for the ancillary services; they have also planned the display of the objects. Mr G. Pearse, assisted by Miss B. K. Wood, has acted as Exhibition Manager since May 1971.

Manuscript documents by Lord Carnarvon and Mr Howard Carter have been lent by the Metropolitan Museum, New York, and the Griffith Institute, Oxford. We are indebted to the governing bodies of these institutions for the loan and to Miss Nora Scott, Curator of the Department of Egyptian Art in the Metropolitan Museum, Miss Helen Murray and Miss Fiona Strachan of the Griffith Institute, for making the documents available to us. Kodak Limited have most generously provided photographic enlargements for display in the forecourt of the Museum.

Transport arrangements have been greatly facilitated by the friendly cooperation of the Ministry of Defence in providing an aircraft of the Royal Air Force to convey about a third of the objects in the exhibition from Cairo to this country. For their considerateness in making these arrangements to meet our needs we are deeply obliged to Mr A. D. Harvey, Air-Commodore W. G. Carr, Mr L. Salthouse and Squadron-Leader J. D. McCrory, all of the staff of the Ministry of Defence. We are also grateful to Mr C. W. Wright (now of the Department of Education and Science) for much advice and assistance at every stage and particularly in our initial discussions with the Ministry of Defence. The remainder of the objects have been brought to this country in two aircraft of the British Overseas Airways Corporation, whose representative, Mr D. E. Bath, has devoted every possible attention to our requirements. The crews of all the aircraft and the police officers who provided the protective escorts for the movement of the objects to and from the air-bases deserve our warmest thanks for the care and courtesy with which they discharged their responsible duties. The expert packing necessary for the transport of the objects has been carried out by Messrs Wingate and Johnston, under the direction of Mr I. A. Pearson, and their agent in Cairo, Mr George Habib. Mr T. G. H. James acted as observer for the sponsors throughout the packing operations.

Dr H. J. Plenderleith, until recently Director of the International Centre for the Study of the Preservation and Restoration of Cultural Property, Rome, went to Cairo in 1970 at the request of the Department of Antiquities of the Egyptian Government to examine the selected objects and to report on their physical condition. As recommended in his report, Mr S. Baker, Senior Conservation Officer in the Department of Egyptian Antiquities in this Museum, visited the Cairo Museum to give assistance in the restoration and consolidation of the golden shrine (no 25), one of the outstanding objects in the exhibition. Dr A. E. Werner, Keeper of the British Museum Research Laboratory, has advised on scientific and technical matters.

The appearance and usefulness of this handbook owe much to those who have designed it and those who have provided the illustrations. Mrs Joy Law, and Mr Alan Bartram have been responsible for the layout. The colour reproductions, with one exception, have been provided by George Rainbird Limited from photographs by Mr F. L. Kenett, apart from no 28 which is by Mr J. Ross. The colour reproduction of no 35 has been kindly supplied by Thames and Hudson Limited, through Mr P. A. Clayton, from a photograph by Mr Albert Shoucair. Very many of the monochrome photographs are the work of the late Mr Harry Burton, the official photographer at the time of the excavation of the tomb; others are by Mr Mohammed Fathy Ibrahim, Mr Sami Mitry and the Smithsonian Institute, Washington. They have been provided by the Griffith Institute, Oxford, the Centre of Documentation, Cairo, the Cairo Museum, the Smithsonian Institute, through Dr D. O'Connor, the Metropolitan Museum, New York, *The Times* and Agence Rapho, Paris. All the line drawings are the work of Mrs Patricia Johnson of this Museum.

In writing the text of the handbook I have been greatly aided by information obtained from Mr Howard Carter's catalogue cards, which are now at the Griffith Institute, Oxford. I am most grateful to the Committee of Management of the Institute for granting me access to them and to the staff of the Institute both for supplying photocopies of the cards and for answering the many queries which I addressed to them.

The staff of this Department, and particularly Mr T. G. H. James, Mr A. F. Shore, Mr S. Baker, Mr J. A. Hayman, Mr M. I. McGrath, Miss C. A. R. Andrews and my personal secretary, Miss A. M. King, have all taken an active part in the preparations for this exhibition. My own debt to them for their constant assistance and support is immeasurable.

I. E. S. EDWARDS
Keeper of Egyptian Antiquities

Tutankhamun, in spite of the almost incredible wealth of material objects discovered in his tomb, still remains a king whose history can be traced only in broken outline. His right to the throne was established, in accordance with Egyptian protocol, through marriage with the princess Ankhesenpaaten, a daughter of the heretic king Akhenaten (c 1379–1362 BC) and his queen Nefertiti. Ankhesenpaaten's elder sister, Merytaten, was already married to Smenkhkare, Akhenaten's co-regent for the last two or three years of his life, who may have been sole ruler for a few months at most. There is no evidence that he left any offspring. Tutankhamun's own parentage is still an unsolved problem. Some authorities believe that he was a son of Akhenaten, but not of Nefertiti, his mother being a minor wife of the king. Others think that he was a son of Akhenaten's father, Amenophis III (c 1417–1379 BC), and a mother who may have been either Amenophis III's principal wife, Tiy, or a lesser wife. Since Tutankhamun was only about nine years of age when he ascended the throne and Akhenaten's reign lasted for about seventeen years, it follows that Tutankhamun could only have been the son of Amenophis III if Akhenaten and Amenophis III were co-regents for at least eight years, and some advocates of this theory favour a longer co-regency, perhaps of twelve years. Much evidence has been adduced by the proponents of both theories, but in the main it is either ambiguous or negative in character. Smenkhkare's parentage is equally uncertain and consequently also his relationship to Tutankhamun. Nevertheless there can be little doubt that both kings were of royal blood and that they had lineal connections with Amenophis III and Akhenaten. They may have been brothers or at least half-brothers.

Tutankhamun (c 1361–1352 BC), or Tutankhaten as he was called for about the first twelve years of his life, was born at a time when Egypt had just undergone an upheaval of a kind which she had not experienced in the whole of her long history. The warrior-kings who reigned in the first hundred and fifty years of the Eighteenth Dynasty, from c 1570 to c 1417 BC, had established their suzerainty over the neighbouring territory northwards far into Syria and southwards beyond the Fourth Cataract of the Nile in the Sudan. As well as much booty acquired in warfare, a steady flow of tribute had come to the country, mainly from the Asian princelings who owed their position to the favour of the pharaohs. Moreover, the natural resources of the country had been greatly developed and the rich gold deposits of Nubia had been fully exploited. No country in the ancient world was so rich in gold as Egypt in the fifteenth century BC and for some time afterwards. Tushratta, king of Mitanni, was merely stating the views of the outside world when he wrote in a letter to the widowed Queen Tiy that in Egypt gold was 'as dust'. Much of this wealth was retained by the king for the royal treasury, but a very substantial amount was assigned to the priesthoods of the temples and, in particular, to the priesthood of Amon-Re in the temple of Karnak at Thebes. By the time of Amenophis III the Karnak priesthood had become the wealthiest body in the land, second only to the crown in its material possessions. To what extent it tried to use the powers which resulted from its affluence for putting pressure on the king in affairs of state cannot be judged, but it is hard to believe that there was not some attempt at interference. There is indeed some evidence that Amenophis II (c 1450–1425 BC) and Tuthmosis IV (c 1425–1417 BC) were conscious of this threat and some of the actions of Amenophis III seem to point unmistakably in that direction.

In Egypt kingship and the rule of the sun-god, with whom Amun (or Amon-Re as he was called at Karnak) was identified, were thought to be inseparable. The king was represented as the divine son of the sun-god and a human mother, ideally the principal wife of his predecessor. Amenophis III, from what we know of his character, would certainly not have been disposed to take direct and drastic action to curtail the temporal powers of the priesthood. He was a pleasure-loving king, who preferred a life of ease, encouraging the arts and building temples to the glory of Amun on a scale which was without precedent. Nevertheless he was the king who was responsible, in every probability, for an innovation and, without doubt, for a development which were to grow in importance until they became paramount in the early stages of the eventual conflict between his son, Amenophis IV (c 1379–1362 BC) and the priesthood of Karnak.

Since time immemorial the temple of Heliopolis had been the centre of the sun-cult in Egypt. It was the sanctuary of the sun-god Re, of whom Re-Horakhty, the sun, and Re-Atum, the force behind the creation of the universe, merely represented different aspects. As an institution, the temple of Heliopolis was bound to the kingship of Egypt by ties which were both historical and religious. But the promotion of the cult of Amon-Re at Karnak from a local to a national status was relatively a recent development, the product of the military and political successes of Amenophis III's predecessors in the Eighteenth Dynasty and of their choice of Thebes, rather than Memphis, to be their capital. The innovation for which Amenophis III seems to have been responsible was the building of a sanctuary in the temple of Karnak to the Heliopolitan Re-Horakhty. His motive in doing so may have been chiefly religious, to bring the older cult into closer connection with the cult of Amon-Re, but it was liable to arouse jealousy from the priesthood of the Theban god and to cause friction between the two sacerdotal bodies. At the same time he gave prominence to another solar entity, the Aten, the name by which the sun itself, and not the god immanent in it, had been known for many centuries. To mention two typical examples, he called the pleasure barge of Queen Tiy 'The Aten gleams' and one of his estates bore the name 'Mansion of the Aten'. Thus used, no deeper meaning need necessarily be attached to the Aten than the 'sun', but in the light of subsequent events it seems more likely that Amenophis III was using it as an anodyne synonym for the name of Re-Horakhty.

If Amenophis III's attitude towards the priesthood of Karnak and their god is still open to speculation, no such uncertainty exists with regard to Amenophis IV. One of his first acts after becoming king was to build a temple at Karnak for Re-Horakhty. To judge from the thousands of decorated blocks which have come to light, this temple, perhaps with later additions, must have covered a very wide area. Re-Horakhty was represented in the same form as at Heliopolis, with the head of a falcon and a human body. There was, however, an important difference: his name was expanded to 'Re-Horakhty, who rejoices in the horizon, in his name the sunlight which is Aten'. Very soon after its earliest occurrence, this name is written in two parts, both enclosed in cartouches like royal names, thereby implying that Amenophis IV regarded Re-Horakhty-Aten as the divine king, although Amon-Re had long borne the epithet 'King of the Gods'.

In order to put in its proper perspective the action of Amenophis IV in building this temple, it should be remembered that some of his predecessors had already built temples at Karnak to gods other than Amon-Re. Tuthmosis III (c 1504–1450 BC), who owed his throne to the priesthood of Karnak, had re-built in stone, near the outer wall of the temple of Amun, an older brick temple to Ptah, the god of Memphis, without alienating the priests of Amun. If Amenophis IV had merely erected a temple to one of the many established deities worshipped in Egypt, it would probably have been tolerated. What he actually did was to build a temple to a transformed Heliopolitan solar deity and elevate him to a higher position than that which had previously belonged to Amon-Re. In a short time even the Heliopolitan link was weakened and Aten, the new deity, was no longer represented in the guise of Re-Horakhty, but as the sun's disk with its rays ending in human hands holding either the hieroglyphic sign for 'life' or the sign for 'dominion' or 'power'. With the introduction of Aten came another innovation – a style of art which was in part naturalistic and in part suggestive of caricature. Some grotesque statues of the king himself which Amenophis IV put in his temple at Karnak illustrate the new style of sculpture in its extreme form. Later in his reign greater emphasis was placed on the naturalistic aspect of the new art, with results which are certainly far more appealing to the modern eye.

Whether or not Amenophis IV imagined, at the beginning of his reign, that the priesthood of Amon-Re would accept his innovations is hard to judge, but at least it is evident that he was not prepared to have an open break with them. His name, which means 'Amun is content', had been given to him at birth, so that it is not necessarily indicative of his initial policy, but a relief in a sandstone quarry at Gebel es-Silsila, which probably dates from his first year on the throne, actually represents him worshipping Amon-Re and shows that he was prepared to pay at least lip-service to the cult. Probably his religious ideas were not at first completely formulated, but, goaded by opposition from the orthodox priesthood and perhaps encouraged by his beautiful wife, Nefertiti, he must very soon have realized that any kind of compromise was incompatible with the fundamental premise of his creed, which was the exclusive character of the Aten, no longer the physical sun but the divine power embodied in it. It was not only Amon-Re who must be suppressed, but the other gods also. Thebes, with its many sanctuaries to different gods, in addition to its traditional ties with Amun, was clearly not the place in which the new religion, the first and the only monotheistic creed in the history of ancient Egypt, could possibly establish itself.

In the fourth year of his reign Amenophis IV, accompanied by Queen Nefertiti, visited the site which, prompted by the Aten, he had chosen for his new capital. It was a crescent-shaped site about eight miles long and three broad, some 240 miles north of Thebes and now known as El-Amarna. The name which he gave to the city was Akhetaten, meaning 'The Horizon of the Aten'. During his visit he issued a proclamation specifying the various buildings which were to be erected there and the tombs which were to be constructed for himself, for Nefertiti, for his daughter Merytaten and for his officials. Two years later the royal family again went to El-Amarna and the king issued another proclamation fixing the boundaries of the city and vowing both that the city would never exceed those boundaries and that the territory thus demarcated would belong to the Aten. A further visit was made in the king's eighth year and by that time it must have been ready for occupation. In the meantime he had changed his name from Amenophis to Akhenaten, which meant 'It is well with Aten', and Nefertiti had added to her name the epithet 'Beautiful is the beauty of Aten' (Neferneferuaten). By this change he had formally dissociated himself from Amun, but his animosity towards the god of his forbears did not end there. He caused the name of Amun to be erased from inscriptions and closed his temples together with the temples of the other gods throughout the land. In addition to the 'Great Temple' and its subsidiaries at El-Amarna, he built sanctuaries dedicated to the Aten at Memphis and elsewhere in Egypt, and at

least one temple in Nubia. Henceforth, insofar as it lay within
Akhenaten's power to control the religious beliefs of his subjects,
Aten ruled not only supreme but in exclusive majesty, and the king was
his high priest through whom the prayers of his adherents were
transmitted to the god. He regarded himself as the apostle of his 'father'
Aten from whom he had received the new creed as though by revela-
tion. As a final act of purification, probably in the ninth year of his
reign, he dropped the name of Horakhty from the designation of Aten
and changed it to 'Re, ruler of the two horizons, who rejoices in the
horizon in his name of Re, the father who has come (again) as Aten'.
Of all the Egyptian pantheon, Re alone had survived, but only because
he was the god in whom the true god, the Aten, had always existed.

   Much of what is known about the rest of Akhenaten's life is derived
from the scenes carved on the walls of the rock-tombs of his courtiers.
The occupations of the royal family, their private and public activities
and, above all, their devotion to the worship of the Aten are repeatedly
depicted; the scenes, however, are all restricted to happenings at
El-Amarna. Nothing is revealed which suggests that the king was
attending to the welfare of his subjects outside the capital. There is
indeed good reason to suspect that the scenes reflect fairly the
limitations of his interests. A possibility which cannot be ignored is
that, until about the twelfth year of his reign, he was merely co-regent,
with Amenophis III still ruling at Thebes, but there is no record at
El-Amarna which suggests a sudden enlargement in his administrative
functions at that time or later. The Amarna Letters, written in
cuneiform and containing the diplomatic correspondence with the
kings of Western Asia and the princelings of Syria and Palestine, show
that he cared little for his inherited responsibilities outside the Nile
Valley. Perhaps Nefertiti appreciated the inevitable consequences to
the throne and to Egypt's economy of her husband's unwillingness to
concern himself with affairs of state and she may have tried to influence
him to change his policy. If, by so doing, she incurred his displeasure,
it might account for the absence of any mention of her name after
about the fourteenth year of Akhenaten's reign. It is possible that she
died, but there is no evidence of it; the excision of her name and even

of her representation on some of the monuments at El-Amarna can easily be explained if she fell out of favour. From that time onwards until Akhenaten's death, in about his seventeenth regnal year, her place is taken by their eldest surviving daughter Merytaten, who married Smenkhkare.

If our conception of the condition of Egypt when Akhenaten died is somewhere near the truth, it is not difficult to imagine some of the problems which faced his successor. Even if Smenkhkare survived his senior co-regent, it was only for a few months, not long enough to effect many changes. That he was a faithful adherent of the cult of Aten is clear from his adoption of 'Beautiful is the beauty of Aten' (formerly Nefertiti's name) as his throne-name. Nevertheless there is documentary evidence that he took some steps to bring about a reconciliation with the priests of Amon-Re, and it is possible that he resided in Thebes during the latter part of his co-regency. Perhaps it was this change of policy which saved the throne for Tutankhaten. At nine years of age he himself could not have done much to influence the course of events, apart from marrying Ankhesenpaaten, who was the crown princess in virtue of being the third of the six daughters of Akhenaten and Nefertiti (the second having died) and the next in age to Smenkhkare's childless wife, Merytaten. The real power must have been held in other hands and there can be little doubt that they were the hands of Ay, who had served Akhenaten as Master of the Horse and was related to the royal family, though it is possible that Nefertiti, if she was still alive, was his active partner. Indirect evidence indicates that the court remained in El-Amarna for the first three years of the young king's reign and then moved to Thebes. Perhaps the move coincided with his ceremonial coronation by the priests of Amon-Re at Karnak, an event which is recorded on some fragments of sculpture. Either then or possibly somewhat earlier he changed his name from Tutankhaten to Tutankhamun (which can be translated either 'Living image of Amun' or 'The life of Amun is pleasing'), and his queen became Ankhesenamun ('She lives for Amun'). They lived, it seems, in the former palace of Amenophis III on the west bank of the Nile, close to Medinet Habu. It was not the only royal residence.

Tutankhamun probably spent much of his time at Memphis, where his administration was centred. The inscription on the handle of the fan, no 23, states that its feathers were obtained by the king when hunting ostriches in the desert east of Heliopolis. It may be a true record of an incident during his life at Memphis. The nominal capital of Egypt was, however, again Thebes and Tutankhamun signified its privileged position by adding to his name the epithet 'Ruler of Southern On', one of the names by which Thebes was known in contrast with the undefined 'On' which was Heliopolis.

A commemorative stela which he set up in the temple of Karnak records some of Tutankhamun's activities and provides a brief but vivid description of the condition of Egypt at the time when he ascended the throne. The temples of the gods and goddesses, from the far south to the Delta, had fallen into decay, their sanctuaries were overgrown with weeds and their halls served as footpaths. Everything was in confusion. If a military expedition went to Syria, it met with no success. The gods had deserted Egypt and the prayers of the people had gone unanswered. Tutankhamun, however, claims that he immediately took action to remedy this melancholy state of affairs. He made costly golden images of 'his father' Amun, of Ptah and of other gods, he built anew their sanctuaries, he re-established their priesthoods and he made lavish gifts to the treasuries of the temples. It is evident from this stela not only that the cult of Amun had been restored to its former position, but that the other gods also had been reinstated. Even Aten was not proscribed, as is shown by the inscriptions on a cabinet in this exhibition (no 15) and on a number of other objects from the tomb which retain the earlier form of his name, Tutankhaten. The counter-revolution was to come later, and eventually the works of 'the enemy of Akhetaten' or 'the Rebel', as Akhenaten was called fifty years after his death, underwent even rougher treatment than he had inflicted on the monuments of Amun.

It is not by chance that the keynote of the only formal record of Tutankhamun's achievements which has yet come to light should be his zeal for the restoration of the old order. It certainly reflects his policy and that of his mentor, Ay. His subjects were given visible proof of his intentions by the interest which he showed in resuming work on monuments which had been left unfinished by Amenophis III at the time of his death. Most conspicuous of all must have been his completion of Amenophis III's entrance colonnade to the temple of Luxor, carving on its walls a record of the most important annual festival at Thebes, the festival of Opet at which the image of Amon-Re was brought by river from Karnak to the temple of Luxor. It is evident that he continued his acts of piety until the end of his life, as a monument in the collection of this Museum proves. It is one of a pair of pink granite lions which Amenophis III intended to place in his newly-built temple at Sulb in Nubia, but the work on the second lion was only in its early stages when he died. Tutankhamun finished the work and put an inscription to that effect on the pedestal. It must have been one of his last undertakings, because an inscription on the breast of the lion records that it was taken to Sulb by his successor Ay.

In view of his age, Tutankhamun is unlikely to have been himself involved in any military operations during his nine years on the throne, though it is probable that he sent an expedition to Palestine and the Lebanon under the command of his General Horemheb, who eventually became Tutankhamun's second successor. Its main purpose seems to have been to bolster the morale of the princelings who had remained loyal to Egypt and whose position was imperilled by a new and warlike neighbour. In the times of Amenophis III and Akhenaten, Tushratta of Mitanni was the most powerful king in western Asia. He was on friendly terms with Egypt and his daughter Tadu-Kheba was one of the wives of Amenophis III. Before the end of Tutankhamun's reign another power, the Hittites, had conquered the Mitanni, and their king, Shuppululiumash, had established his control over the city-states of northern Syria, including some of those which had been nominally Egyptian dependencies. The Hittites, however, had a long-standing treaty with Egypt which they seem to have honoured when it suited them, though it may have helped to prevent them from extending their conquest further south than Damascus and the valley lying between the Lebanon and Antilebanon. Horemheb's expedition could have done nothing to discourage the Hittites, but it seems to have had some beneficial results to Egypt, for there is evidence that once, at least, in his reign Tutankhamun had the satisfaction of receiving rich tribute brought by Asian chieftains. A representation, now badly damaged, of the event is painted on a wall in the tomb of Huy, Tutankhamun's Viceroy of Nubia, together with a similar scene of tribute from Nubia. Perhaps Horemheb had previously led a small military force to Nubia; if so, it could have been little more than a tour of inspection. Nothing suggests that there was any unrest in the South.

Throughout the reign of Tutankhamun the administration of affairs in Egypt was in the hands of the ageing Ay, and his position as head of the government was recognized when the king appointed him to be Vizier. Under Akhenaten temple property, not only of Amun but also of the other gods, had been appropriated by the crown and its restoration to its former owners must have occupied much of Ay's attention in his capacity as Chief Justice, an office which was incorporated in the vizierate. Documentary record of his activities is, however, completely lacking. Among his official duties would certainly have been the preparation of a tomb and the building of a mortuary temple for his royal master. The tomb in which Tutankhamun was eventually buried, by reason of its design and smallness of size, was almost certainly not intended originally for him; very probably Ay had constructed it for himself. A few privileged persons who were not kings, including the parents of Queen Tiy named Yuia and Tjuiu (who were possibly also Ay's parents), had already been buried in the Valley of the Kings and such an honour could have been accorded to Ay in view of his services to Tutankhamun. The tomb intended for Tutankhamun was probably under construction in the western arm of the Valley of the Kings, near the tomb of Amenophis III, when he died prematurely at the age of about eighteen and it could not be completed in time for his funeral. This tomb was later to become Ay's sepulchre. Two statues of Tutankhamun intended for his mortuary temple were found in the mortuary temple of Ay at Medinet Habu.

Neither the examination of his mummy at the time of its discovery nor a more recent examination has established the cause of

Tutankhamun's death. It may have been the result of a head injury suffered in an accident, but, although his skull was damaged near the left ear, it is far from certain that this damage did not occur after his death. It is clear, however, that he died unexpectedly and without issue. Two stillborn children, buried in miniature coffins with Tutankhamun, must have been the offspring of himself and presumably of Ankesenamun, since he is not known to have had any other wife. Considering his age, he might have thought it unnecessary to appoint a co-regent, but there is some evidence that Ay had been promoted to that position and it is he who is shown on the painted walls of Tutankhamun's burial chamber performing the last rites at the youthful king's funeral, a duty which would have been carried out by his eldest son in normal circumstances.

Of Ankhesenamun's fate after her husband's death, nothing is known with certainty; even her tomb has not yet been found, if it still survives. There is, however, in the annals of the Hittite king Shuppiluliumash, a reference to what appears to have been a letter which she had sent to him saying that her husband had died leaving no son and asking him to send one of his sons to marry her. But Shuppiluliumash, surprised by the queen's request, decided to make inquiries lest he should fall into a trap. He therefore dispatched an emissary to Egypt and when the emissary returned he brought a further message from the queen, which satisfied Shuppiluliumash that the request was genuine. The words attributed to her are: 'He will be my husband and king in the country of Egypt'. Thus reassured, Shuppiluliumash complied with her appeal and sent Zannanzash, one of his sons, to Egypt, but he was murdered before he reached his destination. By whom the murder was committed and for what reason, history does not relate. If the record is accepted as it stands, there can be no doubt that the queen who addressed the petition was Ankhesenamun, but the annals of Shuppiluliumash were written many years after his death by his son and second successor, Murshilish, and there is a possibility, since the queen is not mentioned by name, that the letters were sent by Nefertiti after the death of Akhenaten. The name of the husband, as written in the Hittite cuneiform text, is Nipkhururiya, which is the equivalent of the throne-name of Tutankhamun, Nebkheperure, while Akhenaten's throne-name, Neferkheperure, appears in the Amarna letters as Napkhururiya. The difference in the Hittite rendering of the two names is so slight that a mistake in a document written some years after the event had occurred is conceivable.

A possibility, for which the only evidence is a single occurrence on a finger-ring of the names of Ankhesenamun and Ay written side by side, is that Ay married his predecessor's widow in order to legitimize his title to the throne. If so, it was a purely formal marriage of short duration, for his reign did not exceed four years in length. His original wife, Tiy, who had been Nefertiti's nurse, is the only consort who figures in the decoration of his tomb. When Ankhesenamun died, the last lineal descendant, of whom we have any historical knowledge, of some of Egypt's greatest pharaohs had gone. What happened to her three younger sisters is not recorded. One monument has been interpreted as showing that she had already given birth to a daughter by her father Akhenaten before she married Tutankhamun, but, if it is true, the fate of the child is unknown. In her widowhood she may have lived to see Horemheb's misguided attempt to erase the memory of her husband by the usurpation of his monuments, among them the stela at Karnak which recorded his restoration of the temples and the reliefs of the Feast of Opet in the temple of Luxor. Somewhat ironically Horemheb left unharmed the monument which was to bring Tutankhamun far greater fame than he could ever have achieved by his own deliberate effort, though only after some three thousand years. In justice, part of the credit must be accorded to Tutankhamun himself for the encouragement which he gave to the artists and craftsmen who produced the remarkable objects with which his tomb was furnished, but it would have been of no avail if Ay had not surrendered his own tomb to him and if a resolute archaeologist had not, with the help of an enlightened patron, pursued the search for it when the chances of success seemed to others too remote to justify the time and expense.

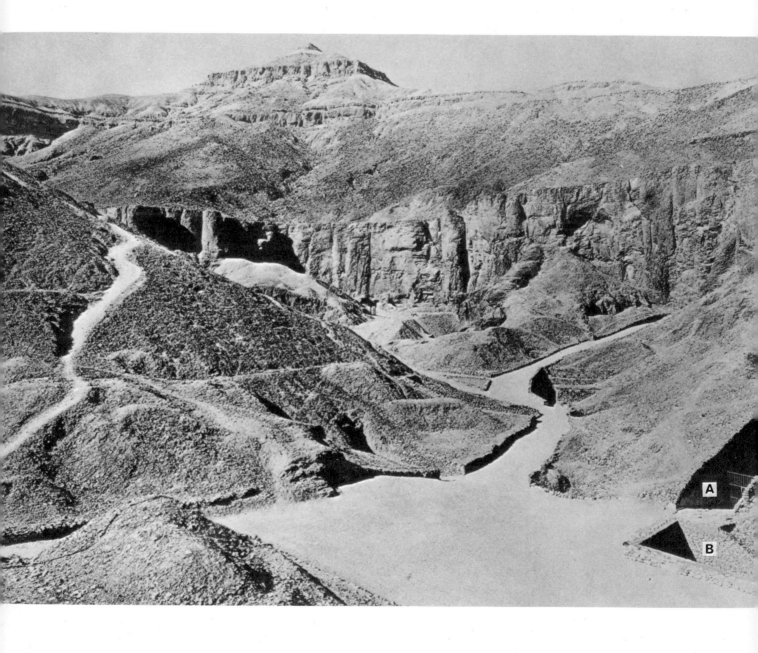

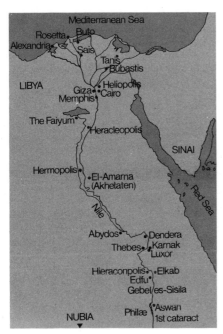

If chance played any part in the discovery of the tomb of Tutankhamun, it was the chance which brought together two men with such different backgrounds as the Earl of Carnarvon and Howard Carter. Lord Carnarvon, born on 26 June 1866, was a collector of rare books and works of art, but he might never have become interested in Egyptology if severe injuries suffered in a motor accident in Germany had not led him to decide on spending the winter months in Egypt for the benefit of his health. Carter, seven years younger than Lord Carnarvon, owed his introduction to Egyptology to a young scholar who was working for the Egypt Exploration Fund on the publication of a group of decorated rock-tombs at Beni Hasan in Middle Egypt. Needing a draughtsman to ink in his tracings of the reliefs and inscriptions in the tombs, the young scholar, later Professor P. E. Newberry, engaged Carter to do the work on the recommendation of Lady Amherst, who had formed a high opinion of Carter's artistic skill. He was then seventeen years of age and he soon showed not only such competence as a draughtsman but also such enthusiasm for the subject-matter of the drawings that, within months of his initiation, he was out in Egypt with Newberry at Beni Hasan. He had his first experience of excavation in the following year, 1892, when he accompanied Sir Flinders Petrie to El-Amarna. Between that date and 1907, when he began his association with Lord Carnarvon, he was employed again by the Egypt Exploration Fund as an archaeological draughtsman in the preparation of a publication of Queen Hatshepsut's temple at Deir el-Bahri, Luxor, and subsequently by the Egyptian government as Inspector of Monuments, first at Luxor and later at Saqqara.

Carter never recorded how it came about that he set his heart on finding the tomb of Tutankhamun, but his work at Luxor gave him plenty of opportunity to form his own opinion about the possibility of making further discoveries in the Valley of the Kings, particularly in the years when, as Inspector of Monuments, he supervised the excavation of two of the tombs found there by Mr Theodore Davis, a rich American patron of Egyptology. That Tutankhamun's tomb was, or at least had been, in the Valley was always a probability.

26

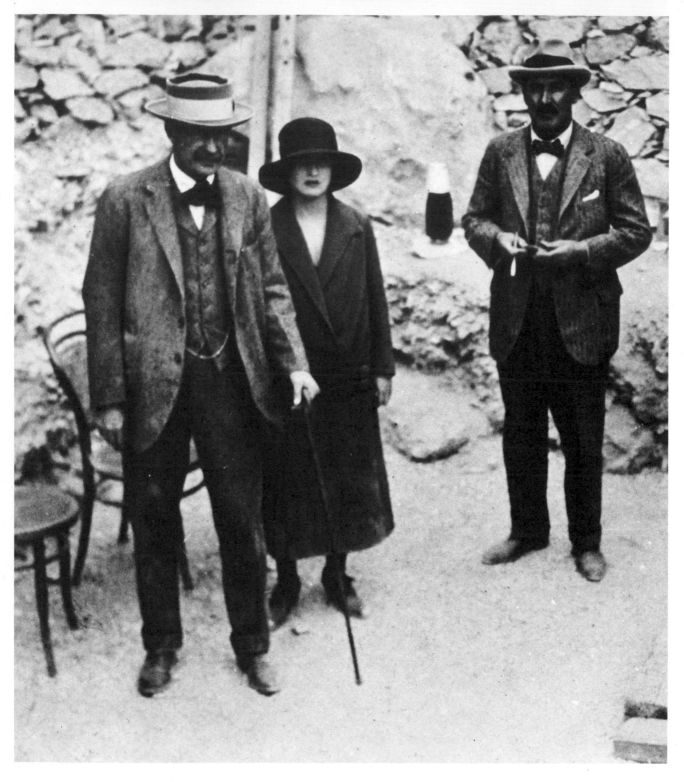

*Lord Carnarvon, Lady Evelyn Herbert*
*and Mr Howard Carter*

Every king from Tuthmosis I (*c* 1525–1512 BC) to Amenophis III (*c* 1417–1379 BC) had been buried there, and so also had Tutankhamun's two successors, Ay and Horemheb. Egyptian kings were usually buried in the cemeteries of their capitals and since Tutankhamun was known to have restored the capital from El-Amarna to Thebes it was likely that he was buried there.

Theodore Davis retained the concession to excavate in the Valley of the Kings until 1914, making many notable discoveries, including the intact tomb of Queen Tiy's parents Yuia and Tjuia, the only intact burial of importance which had ever been found in the Valley. Meanwhile Lord Carnarvon and Carter were working, with less spectacular but useful results, in the neighbourhood of Deir el-Bahri, only a short distance from the Valley on the other side of the cliffs. Carter makes no secret of his impatience to return to the Valley and as soon as Davis relinquished his concession Lord Carnarvon sought and obtained its transfer to himself. It was a mark of confidence in Carter's judgment because Davis, in a publication of what he believed to be the tomb of Tutankhamun, had written two years previously 'I fear that the Valley of the Tombs (of the Kings) is now exhausted'. Giovanni Belzoni had expressed a similar opinion, a century earlier, but with less justification than Davis.

What Davis had identified in 1907 as the tomb of Tutankhamun was in fact a discovery of considerable interest, but it was not the tomb. It was a small underground chamber filled with dried mud which yielded an uninscribed alabaster figure and a broken wooden box with some pieces of gold leaf embossed with the names of Tutankhamun, Ankhesenamun and Ay. In the light of subsequent events it became evident that these objects had been stolen in antiquity from the real tomb of Tutankhamun and hidden in the chamber. A faience vessel inscribed with Tutankhamun's name, which Davis found under a large boulder in the vicinity, must be explained in the same way.

Not far from the underground chamber Davis made another discovery of far greater significance, but to which he attached little importance. It was a pit containing about a dozen large white pottery jars filled with linen, some of it marked with the name of

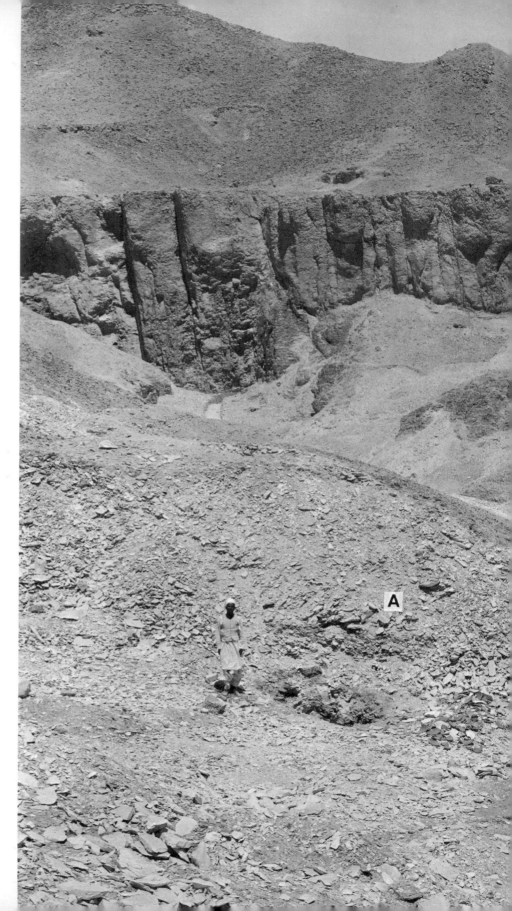

28 *Pit found by Mr Theodore Davis containing the material used in embalming Tutankhamun* (A) *and the position of the tomb of Tutankhamun* (B)

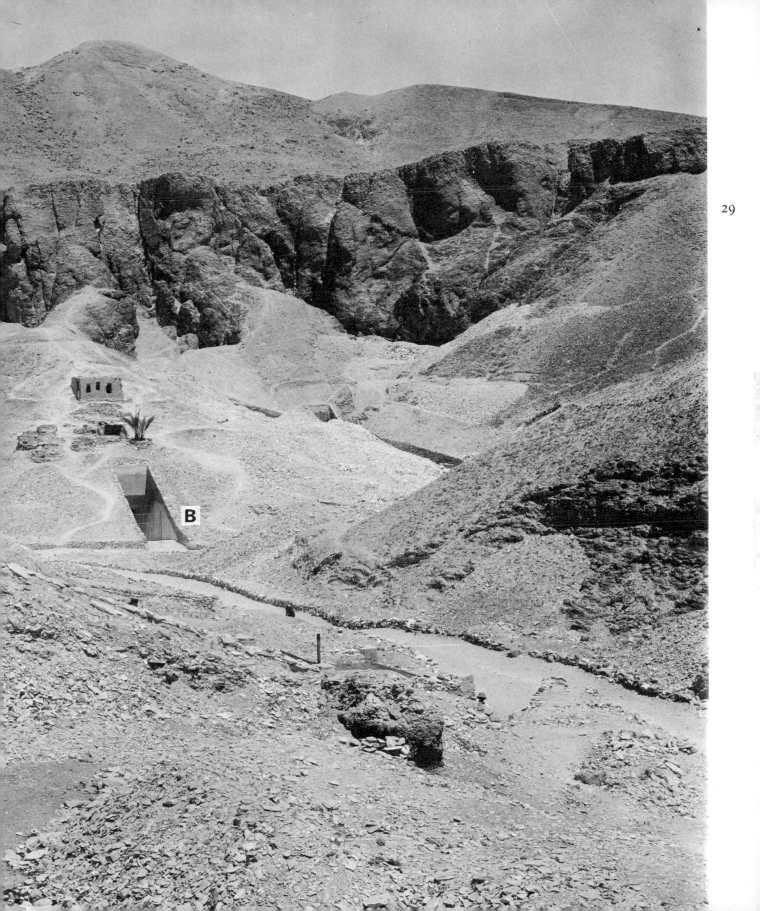

30

Tutankhamun, bags of chaff, bags of natron, a small anthropoid mask made of plaster and linen, many different kinds of pots, some of which had been deliberately broken, bones of birds and animals, some floral collars and two brooms. Eventually Davis gave most of these objects to the Metropolitan Museum, New York, where they were studied by Mr Herbert Winlock, the Curator of the Egyptian Department. Davis supposed that they represented the contents of a small tomb robbed in antiquity, which the ancient necropolis guards had collected and reburied in the pit. It was Winlock who realized that they had a far greater interest: they were in part the materials

*Floral collar worn by a guest at Tutankhamun's funerary banquet from the pit shown on page 28; and (opposite) bags of natron and chaff used in the mummification of Tutankhamun*

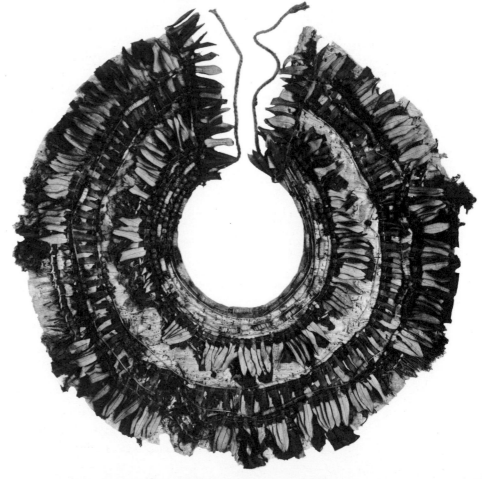

which had been used by the embalmers when mummifying the body of
Tutankhamun and in part the relics of the banquet, attended by about
eight people, held, in accordance with custom, at the time of
Tutankhamun's funeral.

Winlock did not publish the results of his study until long after the
tomb of Tutankhamun had been found, but he communicated his
conclusions to Carter. They transformed what had previously been a
probability into a virtual certainty: Tutankhamun must have been
buried in the Valley. Even so, there was no proof that his tomb had
survived in a recognizable condition. The Valley with its side branches

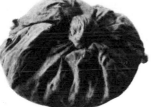
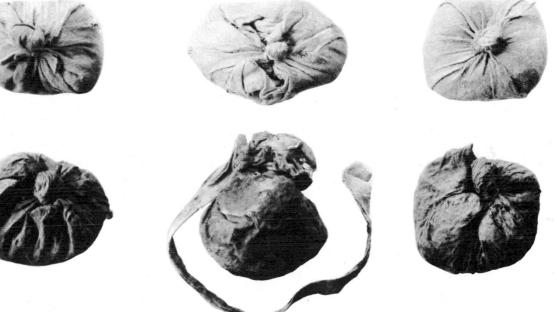

was of considerable size and everywhere lay vast piles of sand and
rock, the dumps of earlier excavators, with no guarantee that the
ground beneath had been properly examined before being covered.
With the help of present-day mechanical equipment the removal of the
dumps would not have presented serious difficulties, but it was not
available in Carter's time. The only tool was the adze and the only

32

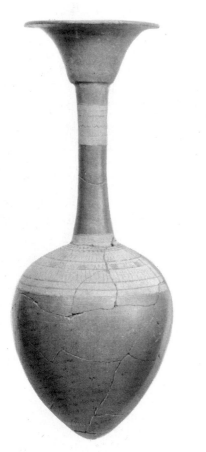

*A pottery vessel found in the pit on page 28*

method of transport was by basket either to a new dump nearby or to trucks on rails for conveyance to a dump farther away. Manpower, however, was plentiful and not expensive.

Undaunted by the prospect of a long and arduous search, Lord Carnarvon and Carter made their preparations to explore the Valley down to bed-rock, but scarcely had work begun when it was interrupted by the First World War and it was not resumed until 1917. Season after season it was continued with results which were so meagre that it is doubtful whether any public organization would have felt justified in continuing the work. After six seasons even Lord Carnarvon came to the conclusion that the returns were not commensurate with the cost. Some 200,000 tons of sand and rubble had been removed without bringing to light a single object of importance. A small cache of alabaster vessels inscribed with the names of Ramesses II (c 1304–1237 BC) and his son Merneptah (c 1236–1223 BC) was almost the only discovery recorded. He knew, however, that Carter's faith in ultimate success was not greatly shaken by what he himself later described as the 'extremely scanty results' of the work. By the summer of 1922 he had made up his mind to terminate the excavations. He therefore asked Carter to visit him at Highclere, his residence near Newbury, and explained to him his decision. Carter was prepared for it and had his answer ready. Pulling out a plan of the Valley, he showed Lord Carnarvon that there was one small area at the foot of the approach to the tomb of Ramesses VI (c 1156–1148 BC) which they had not examined in their first full season because by doing so they would have prevented visitors from reaching the tomb, and he proposed that the search should be continued for one more season in that region, on the understanding that he himself would bear the cost if the results were again disappointing. Lord Carnarvon was so touched by Carter's offer that he immediately agreed to let him have his way, but on the same terms as in the past. As events were to prove, it was a fateful decision for both of them.

Leaving England in time to reach Egypt before the usual influx of foreign visitors, Carter was ready to begin his excavations on

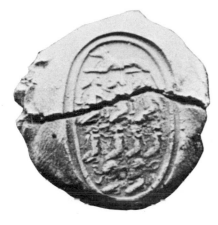

1 November 1922, just outside the entrance to the tomb of Ramesses VI. On the first day he uncovered a group of workmen's huts, some of which he had already located five years previously. They stood about three feet above bed-rock and Carter's first task was to prepare a plan of them. When he arrived on the dig on the morning of 4 November his men had removed the first hut, together with the underlying sand, and had uncovered a step cut in the rock-floor of the Valley. By the next day they had uncovered twelve steps, without reaching the bottom of the stairway but revealing the upper part of a doorway which must lead to a tunnel in the rock; the doorway was blocked, plastered over and marked with impressions of the seal of the ancient necropolis guards – a recumbent jackal over the figures of nine foreign captives. Had he really found the tomb of Tutankhamun? Whatever it was, it was clear that no one had penetrated the doorway at least since the workmen's huts had been built, and they had belonged to the men who were employed on the construction of the tomb of Ramesses VI. Nothing more could be done until Lord Carnarvon, who was still in England, had been informed, and so on the morning of 6 November Carter sent his historic cable: 'At last have made wonderful discovery in the Valley; a magnificent tomb with seals intact; re-covered same for your arrival; congratulations.'

Carter had made his discovery within a few feet of the point at which his excavations had stopped in 1917–18 and about 120 yards from the pit in which Davis had found the jars containing the material used by Tutankhamun's embalmers and the remains of the funeral feast.

On 23 November Lord Carnarvon, accompanied by his daughter Lady Evelyn Herbert, reached Luxor and on the next day the entire staircase of sixteen steps was cleared. There, beyond any doubt, on the lower part of the blocking of the doorway, were the impressions of the seal of Tutankhamun. A disconcerting feature, however, was the discovery that the seal impressions of the necropolis authorities were placed on what was clearly not the original blocking, whereas the seal-impressions of Tutankhamun were on the original plaster. Evidently the tomb had been entered by thieves at some time before the reign of Ramesses VI and had been re-closed by the necropolis officials. It

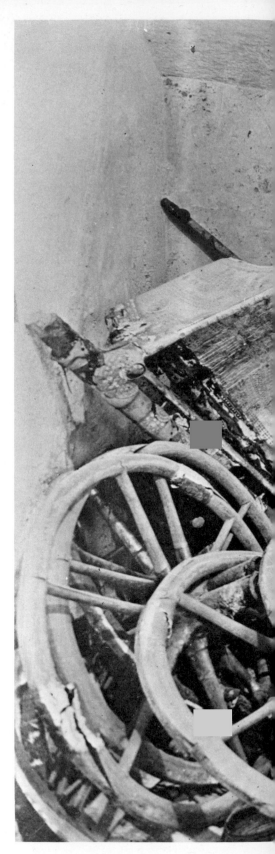

34  explained the small cache of objects which Davis had found in the underground chamber not far away, but it was a disappointment to the two excavators who had been hoping to find the tomb intact. Nevertheless it was reasonable to suppose that the necropolis officials would not have restored the blocking if nothing had remained to be protected.

After the seal-impressions had been photographed, the blocking, consisting of stones faced on the outer side with plaster, was removed. Beyond lay a sloping tunnel completely filled from floor to roof with stones and rubble, but again showing evidence of restoration after penetration by thieves. Thirty feet along the tunnel was a second doorway, blocked like the first and similarly marked with the seal impressions of Tutankhamun and the necropolis authorities. By the afternoon of 26 November everything was ready for taking down the blocking. With Lord Carnarvon, Lady Evelyn Herbert and his assistant Mr Callender standing beside him, Carter prised out some of the stones at the top and inserted a candle through the hole. What happened in the next few moments can only be described in Carter's own words: 'At first I could see nothing, the hot air escaping from the chamber causing the candle to flicker, but presently, as my eyes grew accustomed to the light, details of the room within emerged slowly from the mist, strange animals, statues, and gold – everywhere the glint of gold. For the moment – an eternity it must have seemed to the others standing by – I was struck dumb with amazement, and when Lord Carnarvon, unable to stand the suspense any longer, inquired anxiously "Can you see anything?" it was all I could do to get out the words "Yes, wonderful things".' He was gazing into the Antechamber and among the objects which he could see were several of the pieces shown in this exhibition, including the cow-bed, the large gilded wooden statue, the chair and some of the chests. It was no exaggeration when he wrote: 'Surely never before in the whole history of excavation had such an amazing sight been seen as the light of our torch revealed to us.' For him 26 November 1922, was 'the day of days, the most wonderful that I have ever lived through, and certainly one whose like I can never hope to see again.'

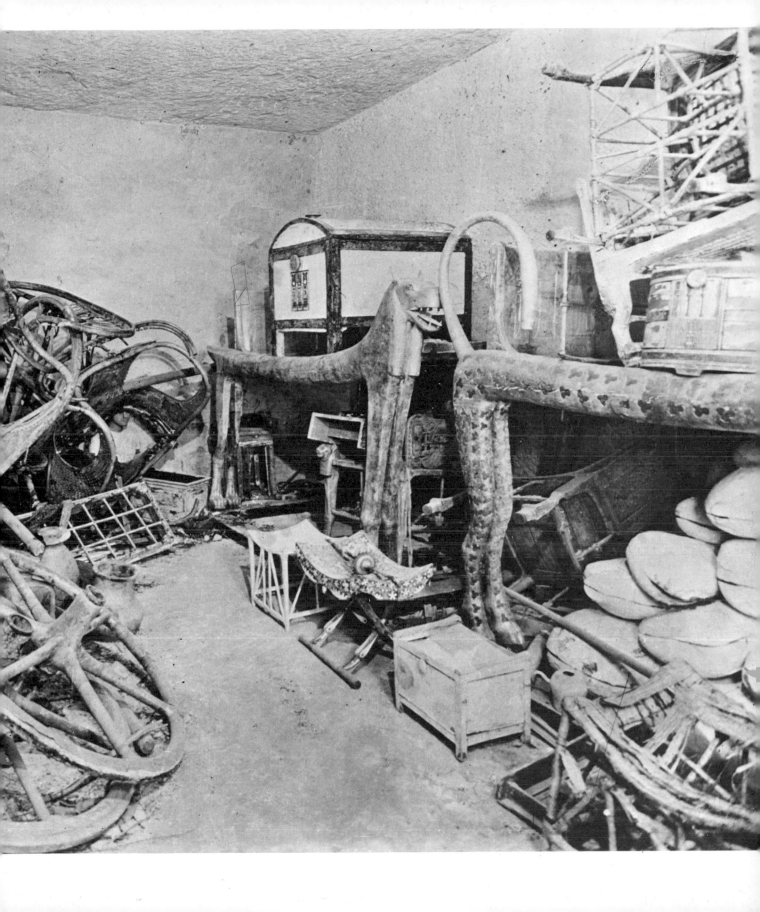

# The tomb and its discovery

*Queen Elisabeth of the Belgians (seated at the entrance) visiting the tomb*

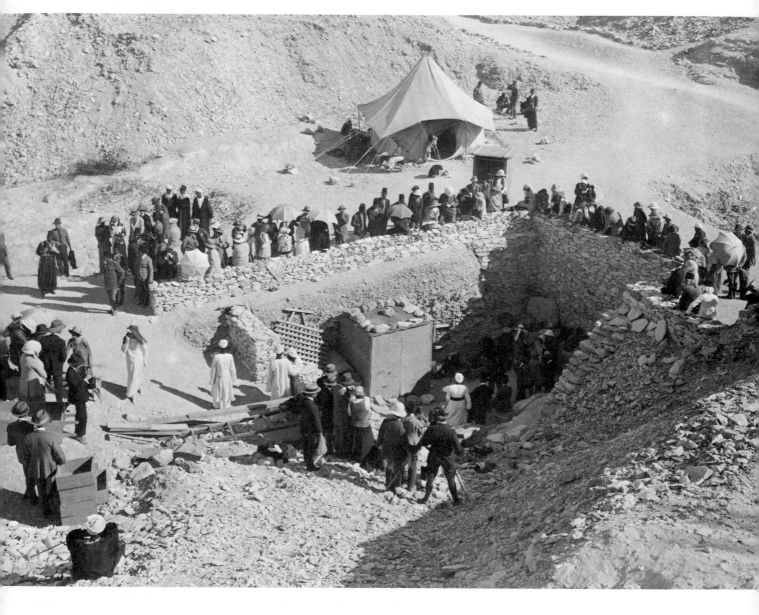

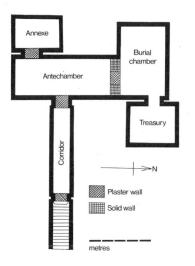

Annexe

Burial chamber

Antechamber

Corridor

Treasury

N

Plaster wall

Solid wall

metres

What Lord Carnavon and Carter had seen that day was only a small   37
part of the entire contents of the tomb, but it was enough to convince
them that, in spite of the efforts of the ancient robbers, the outcome of
their long search was bound to surpass their wildest dreams. Very soon
they were to discover three more chambers, one containing the
mummified body of the king, his head completely enveloped in the
astonishing gold portrait mask displayed in this exhibition (no 50).
There he lay, untouched since the day of burial, in an anthropoid coffin
of solid gold which alone weighed approximately 296 pounds troy
(110.4 kilograms). It was the innermost of three coffins, similar in
style and fitting tightly, one inside another, but the middle and
outermost coffins were not made of gold; they were carved of wood
and overlaid with gold, the feather decoration of the middle coffin
being encrusted with polychrome glass and semi-precious stones. A
massive quartzite rectangular sarcophagus, its lid of granite cracked
and repaired with plaster, enclosed the three anthropoid coffins.
Exactly fitting the sarcophagus was the smallest of four floorless
wooden shrines, one inside another, all overlaid with thin gold
embossed with magical texts and figures of protecting deities

Although the thieves had broken into the burial chamber, they had
not attempted to reach the mummy, not out of respect for the
deceased but merely because it could not be done in the short time
before their activities were stopped. Thus, for the first time in history,
it was possible to see how an ancient Egyptian pharaoh was buried.
Many mummies of kings had been found previously, but only one, the
mummy of Amenophis II, was in its original tomb, and all of them had
been robbed of the valuable articles which had been buried with them.
In the case of Tutankhamun not only had his mummy, and all the
treasures immediately associated with it, survived intact, but also a
vast amount of the rest of his tomb-equipment, including very many of
his personal possessions. Most of the objects, apart from the Ushabti
figures, are without parallel, so that it is very difficult to form an
opinion on how they compared in quality with the tomb-equipment of
his mightier predecessors and successors in the Eighteenth and
Nineteenth Dynasties. In the few instances in which comparison is

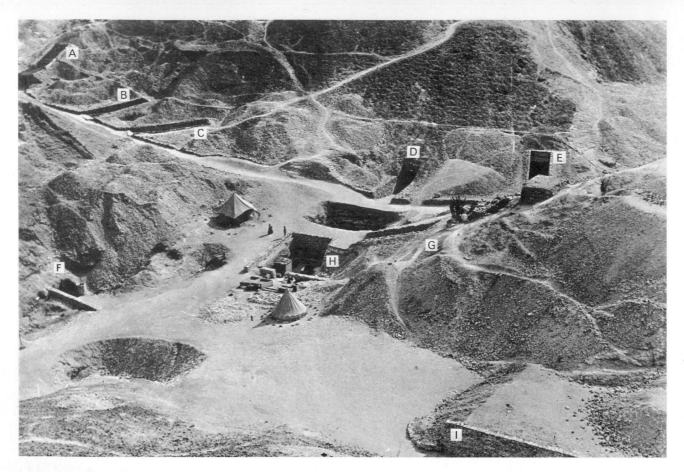

(Above) Royal tombs around the tomb of
Tutankhamun. (A) Ramesses X,
(B) Sethos I, (C) Ramesses I,
(D) Amenmesses, (E) Ramesses III,
(F) 'Tomb of Queen Tiy', (G) Ramesses VI,
(H) Tutankhamun and (I) Merneptah.
(Opposite above) Field laboratory in the
tomb of Sethos II; (opposite below)
Wrapping a wooden statue of
Tutankhamun

possible, the impression given is that the objects buried with
Tutankhamun were both richer and finer. Certainly many of them
display a level of workmanship and technical skill which is almost
unbelievable. Many also are works of art which bear comparison with
the finest products of the ancient world, particularly in representa-
tional art. The exaggerated style of the early Amarna age had
developed into a more truly naturalistic form of representation which
even the restrictions of convention and the absence of perspective, in
the case of two dimensional works, could not obscure. Among the
many examples of this very subtle artistic achievement which can be
seen in this exhibition, perhaps the most outstanding are the gold
mask and the gilded figure of the king harpooning, some of the scenes
on the small gold shrine, the reliefs of the ostrich hunt on the palm of
the fan and the scene of the king fowling, with the queen at his side, on
the carved ivory overlay of a casket.

If the element of chance played little part in the discovery of the
tomb, it was undoubtedly a major factor both in determining the use to
which the tomb was put in the first instance and in its subsequent
preservation. Tutankhamun was buried there and not in the tomb
which was being prepared for him elsewhere because his intended

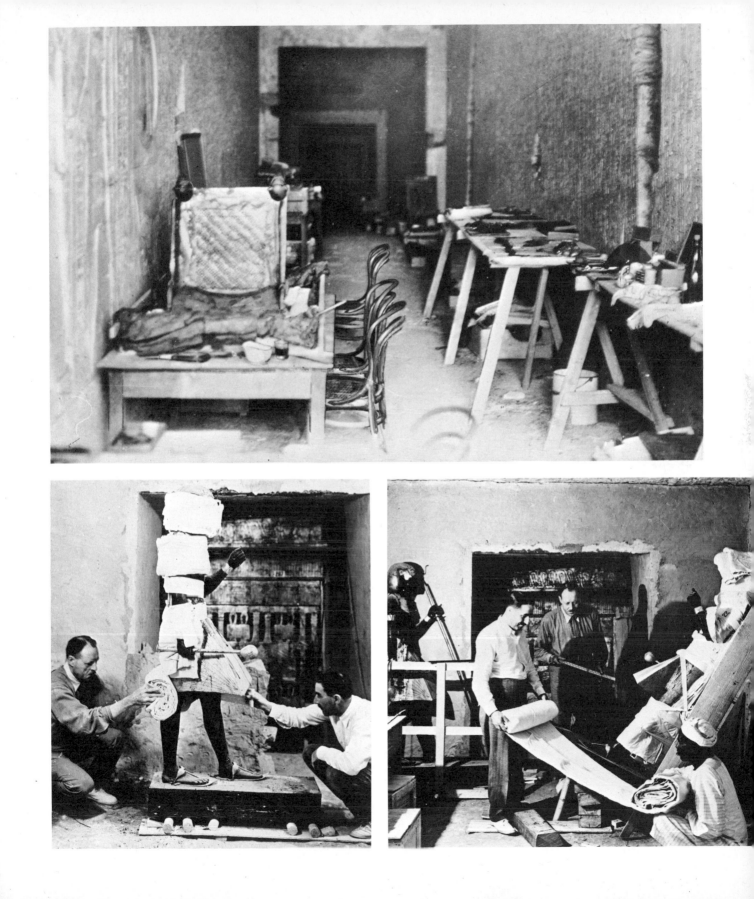

tomb was not ready at the time of his premature death. Its entrance was already 'lost' under three feet of sand when Ramesses VI decided to hew out a tomb for himself in the face of the rock just above Tutankhamun's tomb. The rubble extracted in the process must have been left nearby until after the funeral of Ramesses VI and then it was used to conceal the entrance to his tomb. Being so placed some of it was on top of Tutankhamun's tomb, thus burying it still deeper. From that moment the chances of discovery were small, but two centuries lay between the reigns of Tutankhamun and Ramesses VI and the exact whereabouts of Tutankhamun's tomb must have been known to a large number of people for some time after his death and, in particular, to the community of workmen who were permanently employed in the necropolis. That such workmen were not always reliable is certain. A papyrus in the collection of this Museum reports an investigation in which eight of the workmen engaged on the construction of the tomb of Ramesses IX were found to have committed thefts from the tomb of Queen Ese, wife of Ramesses III. Some of their predecessors in the community may well have been the robbers who tunnelled their way into the tomb of Tutankhamun. Whoever they were, the fact that they were not able to recover the objects which they had hidden in the underground chamber found by Davis suggests that they were quickly apprehended. If, as Carter believed, the robbery occurred soon after Tutankhamun's burial, prompt action to deal with it would no doubt have been taken by Maya, the Superintendent of Building Works in the Necropolis who contributed the small effigy (no 10) and some Ushabti figures to the king's funerary equipment. Maya continued to hold this office, together with other posts to which he had been promoted, for many years after Tutankhamun's death, at least until the eighth year of Horemheb and probably longer. By the time he ceased to be in charge of the necropolis, one of the violent rainstorms which, at long intervals, descend on the Valley, turning it into a sea of mud, may well have left the entrance to the tomb completely indistinguishable from the surrounding terrain. Such a development would have been greatly facilitated by its being in the floor of the Valley instead of on the rising face of the rock. It seems, therefore, that its

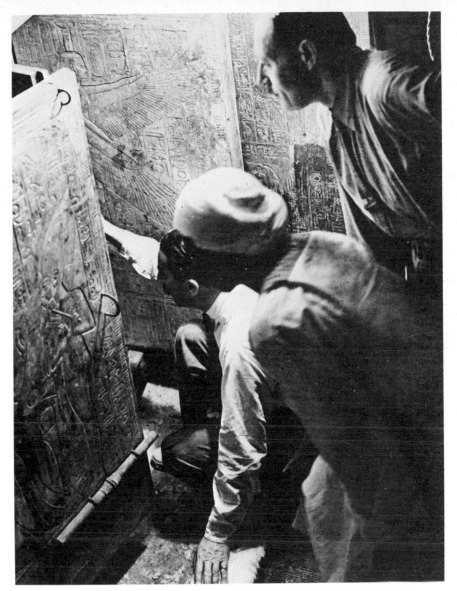

*Opening the doors of the fourth and innermost shrine*

survival was due, in the first place, to fairly effective official supervision during the period immediately after the burial, followed by the action of natural forces which obscured the outward and visible traces of its existence, and lastly to the stroke of good fortune by which Ramesses VI constructed his own tomb only a few feet away.

In the course of his excavations, Carter was able to observe how the robbers had made their entry into the tomb and also to form an opinion on what they had stolen. It was evident that the tomb had been violated twice. On the first occasion the entrance passage between the two blocked doorways must have been clear because Carter found fragments of objects from the tomb buried under the filling when he was taking it out. On the second occasion the filling had been introduced so that the robbers had to dig a small tunnel immediately

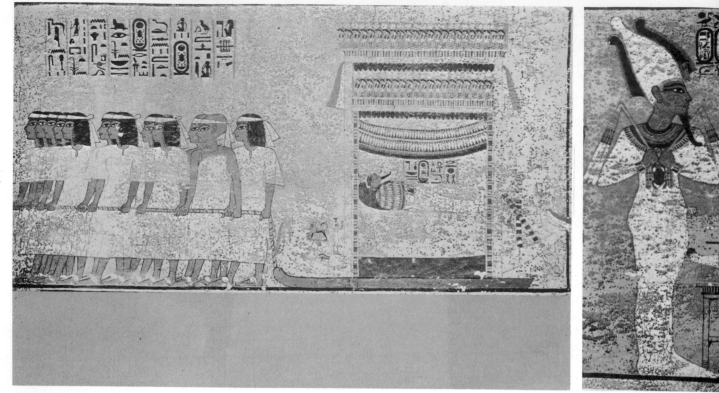

42

*The wall paintings around the Burial Chamber. East wall: Tutankhamun's mummy lying on a leomorphic bier within two shrines and watched over by Isis (stern) and Nephthys (bows) is towed to the tomb by twelve courtiers. The shrines are mounted on a funerary boat which has been placed on a sledge for dragging over land. The action is described in the hieroglyphic inscription above the courtiers*

under the ceiling of the passage and against the left wall. The first plunderers were chiefly interested in portable objects made of gold, silver and bronze, whereas the second gang concerned themselves mainly with the costly oils and unguents stored in the alabaster vessels. There was no space to take the vessels through their tunnel, so they emptied the contents into water-skins; the finger-marks of one of the thieves were still visible on the interior of a vessel which had contained a viscous ointment. Among the metal objects stolen were the gold figure of the king, and probably of the queen also, from the small shrine in this exhibition (no 25), the bronze heads of arrows and the bits from bridles. Several gold finger-rings which the thieves had intended to take were left behind, wrapped up in a piece of linen, perhaps because they had to leave in a hurry.

When the robberies were discovered, officials entered the tomb and made some attempt to restore order, but their work was very perfunctory. Lids of chests which had been wrenched off by the thieves were still left on top of other pieces of furniture where they had been thrown. Their contents, which must have been strewn about the floor, were simply put back in the chests without regard to whether or not they corresponded with the articles listed in the inventories written on the lids of some of the chests. In this respect the officials who placed the objects in the tomb at the time of Tutankhamun's funeral were not

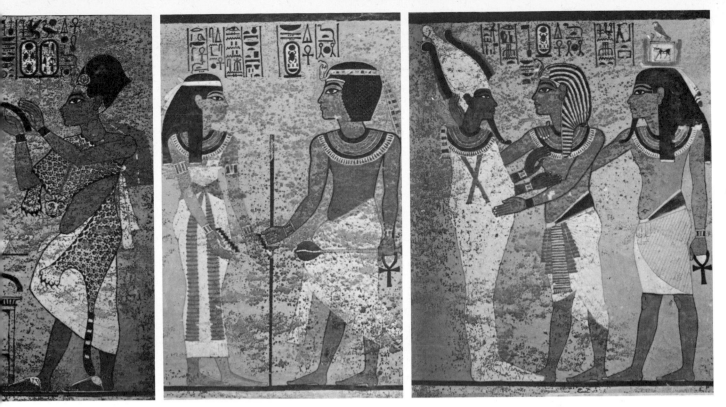

always as fastidious as they might have been, but some consistency
could be detected in what appears to be their carelessness. More than
half the boxes containing food which were stacked under the cow-bed
were labelled with their supposed contents, but in only a very few
instances did the actual contents prove to be the articles stated on the
label. Nevertheless, within any group of boxes bearing the same label,
the joint of meat or the fowl which had been put in each box, although
it did not agree with the label, was generally identical. Such a degree of
consistency suggests that the labels were written in advance and the
particular item was not available at the time when the boxes were
filled.

It is not hard to imagine that haste was just as imperative for the
restorers as it was for the robbers. The longer the tomb was left
unsealed, the greater would be the risk of further robbery, and also
greater attention would be drawn to its exact location. Having quickly
put back wherever they found room the objects which were lying on
the floor, they repaired the hole made by the robbers in the partition-
wall between the Antechamber and the Burial Chamber and then
repeated the operation on the blocking of the inner and outer
doorways, filling in the robbers' tunnel as they moved backwards
towards the staircase. If Carter was right in his estimate that a chain of
men passing back baskets of earth and rubble could have hollowed

*North wall: (far left) King Ay, wearing the
leopard skin of a setem-priest performs the
Opening of the Mouth ceremony on
Tutankhamun who is represented as Osiris;
(centre) the goddess Nut greets her son,
king Tutankhamun; (right) Tutankhamun
accompanied by his double (ka) embraces
the god Osiris, lord of the West.*

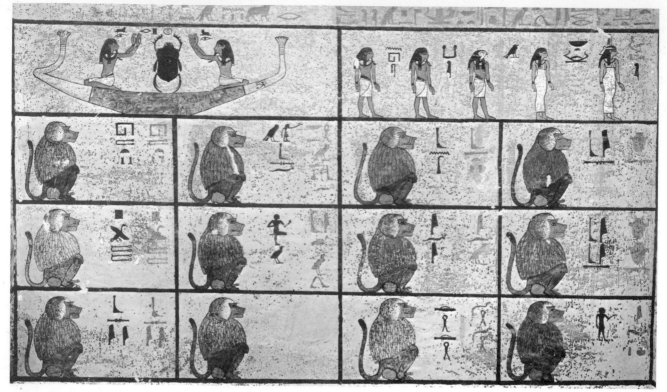

*West wall: (above) Deities of the first hour
of the Book of what is in the Underworld.
South wall: (opposite) Hathor holds the
symbol of life to the nostril of Tutankhamun.
Behind him stands Anubis.
(Right below) The outermost coffin lying in
the sarcophagus*

out the tunnel in seven or eight hours, the entire work of restoration
need not have occupied longer than a day. It must have been a
laborious task, but it achieved its purpose. For more than three
thousand years the treasures which they had saved remained
untouched in the tomb.

The task which confronted Carter when he made the discovery was
enormous and far greater than he could possibly accomplish with the
help of only one assistant, Mr A. R. Callender. Every object had to be
scientifically recorded and photographed before it could be moved
from the tomb, and much conservation work was also necessary. A
further problem was the transport of all the treasures from the Valley
of the Kings to the Cairo Museum, a journey of more than four
hundred miles involving, in its early stages, carriage over five and a
half miles of uneven terrain to the river bank. He did not have to go
far for help. Through the generosity of the authorities of the Metropolitan Museum, New York, whose expedition was working nearby at
Deir el-Bahri, he was granted the services of two draughtsmen, Mr
Lindsley F. Hall and Mr Walter Hauser, an archaeologist, Mr A. C.
Mace and a photographer, Mr Harry Burton, many of whose
photographs are reproduced in the illustrations of this handbook.
Professor P. E. Newberry, to whom Carter owed his introduction to
Egyptology, and Dr A. H. (later Sir Alan) Gardiner undertook all the

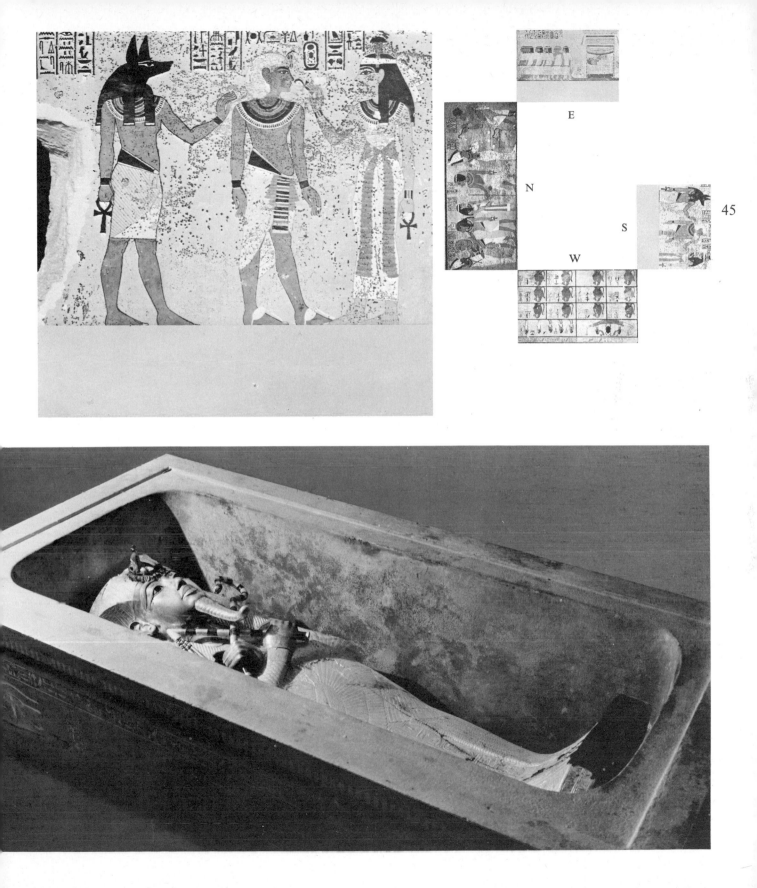

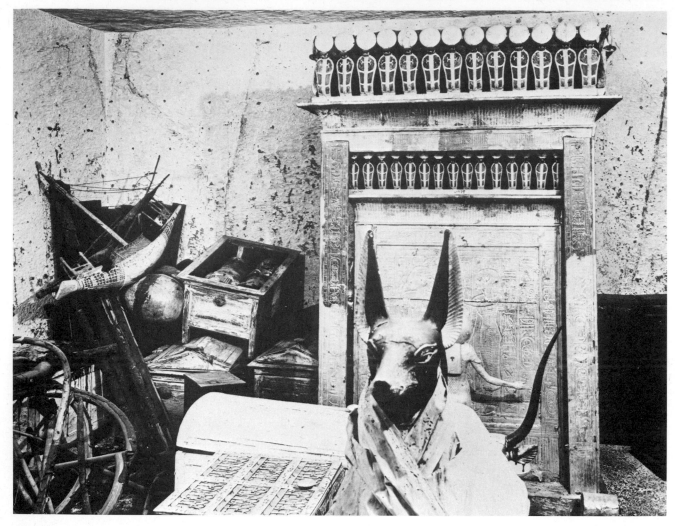

*First view of the Treasury*

epigraphic work, and Mr Alfred Lucas, then Director of the Chemical Department of the Egyptian Government and subsequently Honorary Consulting Chemist of the Service of Antiquities, was responsible both for giving scientific advice on moving objects from the tomb and for the conservation of the many pieces which were in a weak condition through decay or other causes, so that they could travel to Cairo without risk of further injury. Setting up a field laboratory in the tomb of Sethos II (*c* 1216–1210 BC), he discharged his difficult task most skilfully and much of the credit for the successful completion of Carter's labours is due to him.

If the discovery had been made at the present time, it would have been possible to transport the objects on a tarmac road from the Valley of the Kings to the river or perhaps by helicopter to Luxor airport on the east bank, but fifty years ago no such amenities existed. Carter had to choose between transport by camel, by porters and by Décauville railway and he decided on the railway. The operation

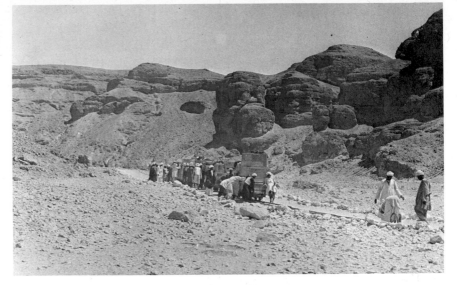

would not have been difficult if he had possessed enough track to cover the distance, but his supply amounted to no more than a few lengths of railway line which had to be lifted, after the trucks loaded with boxes of objects had been pushed forward over them, and relaid farther forward in readiness for the next move. With a gang of fifty men a rate of more than a third of a mile an hour was maintained and the whole journey from the tomb to the river bank occupied no longer than fifteen hours. Carried out in the heat of summer with iron rails which were almost too hot to touch, it was a very remarkable achievement. Seven days after the boxes were loaded on a steam vessel belonging to the Antiquities Service of the Egyptian Government they were safely delivered to the Cairo Museum.

The clearance of the tomb occupied Carter and his helpers for ten years. By then he was sixty years of age and in poor health, with the consequence that he was never able to undertake the scientific publication of the vast quantity of priceless material which his efforts had brought to light, although he wrote a popular account of the discovery in three volumes, the first with his assistant A. C. Mace as joint author. Seven years later, on 2 March 1939, he died in London. His patron, Lord Carnarvon, had died in Cairo on 6 April 1923, as a result of pneumonia following a blood infection, the outcome of a mosquito bite at Luxor. Tutankhamun, the young king whose memory the two excavators had so dramatically immortalized, was left in his tomb enclosed in the outermost of the three coffins which protected his mummy. Apart from this coffin and the quartzite sarcophagus in which it was placed, all the furniture of the tomb went to the Cairo Museum where it occupies two whole galleries. The fifty pieces shown in this exhibition, although numerically only a small part of the entire collection, include many of its finest treasures.

# THE EXHIBITS

1 Wooden statue of Tutankhamun
2 Model boat
3 Floral unguent vase
4 Leomorphic unguent vase
5 Painted casket
6 The god Ptah
7 Lotiform chalice
8 Stopper from the Canopic chest
9 Canopic coffin
10 Miniature effigy of the king
   lying on a bier
11 Ushabti figure
12 Gilded cow's head
13 Bed of the divine cow
14 Portable chest
15 Ornate cabinet
16 Child's chair and footstool
17 Bow-fronted box
18 Gaming board
19 Ivory palette of Merytaten
20 Ornate stool
21 Ornamented chest
22 Gold figure of the king
23 Ostrich feather fan
24 Emblem of Anubis
25 Golden shrine
26 Gilded statuette of the king
27 Tutankhamun, the harpooner
28 Statuette of the king upon a leopard
29 Amuletic collar
30 Pectoral with solar and lunar emblems
31 Necklace with triple scarab pectoral
32 Necklace of the rising sun
33 Necklace of the sun on the eastern
   horizon
34 Decorated scarab
35 Scarab bracelet
36 Gold dagger and sheath
37 Head-rest
38 Royal sceptre
39 Earrings
40 Vulture collar
41 Amuletic collar
42 Necklace with winged scarab pectoral
43 Necklace with vulture pendant
44 Crook and flail
45 Trumpet
46 Squatting figure of a king
47 Miniature coffin
48 Boomerang
49 Decorated bow
50 The gold mask

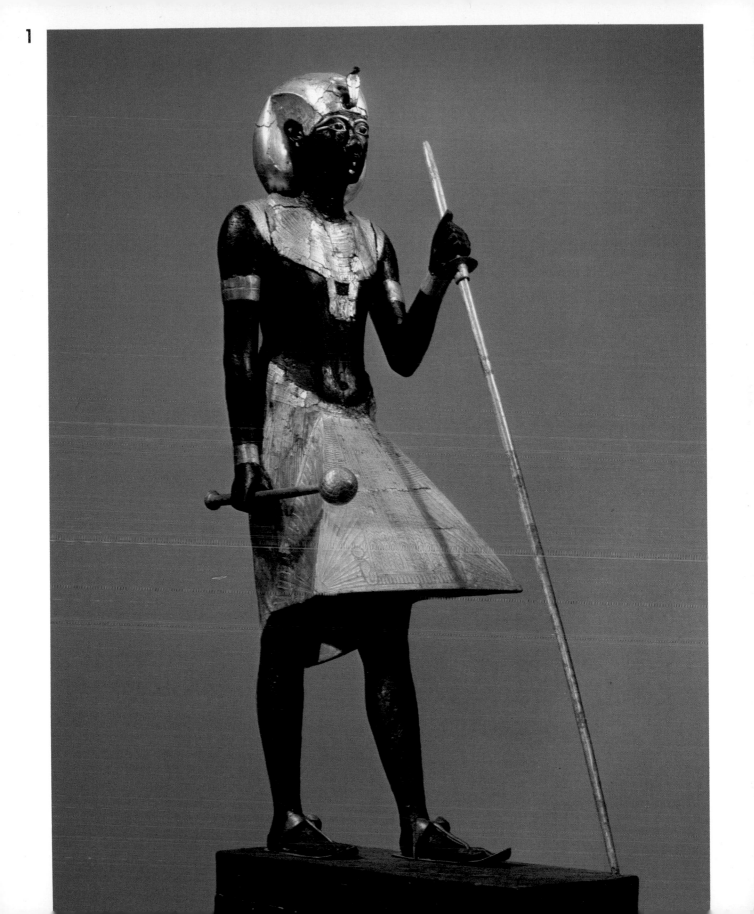

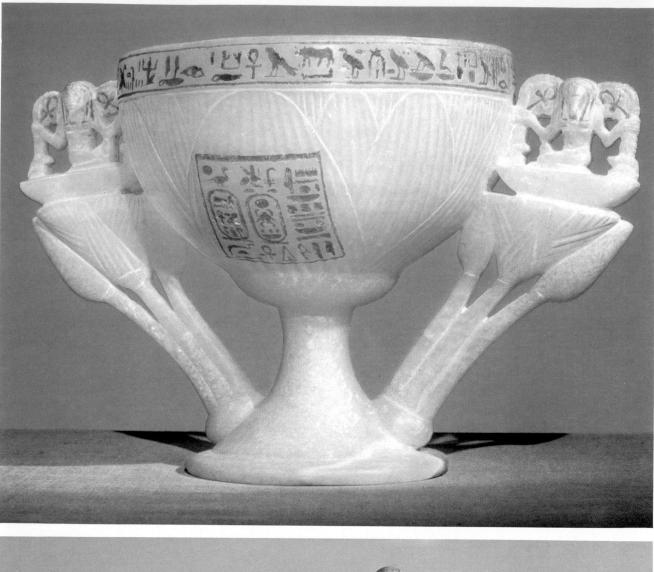

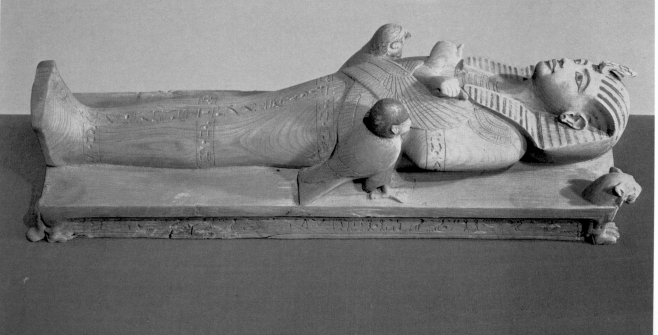

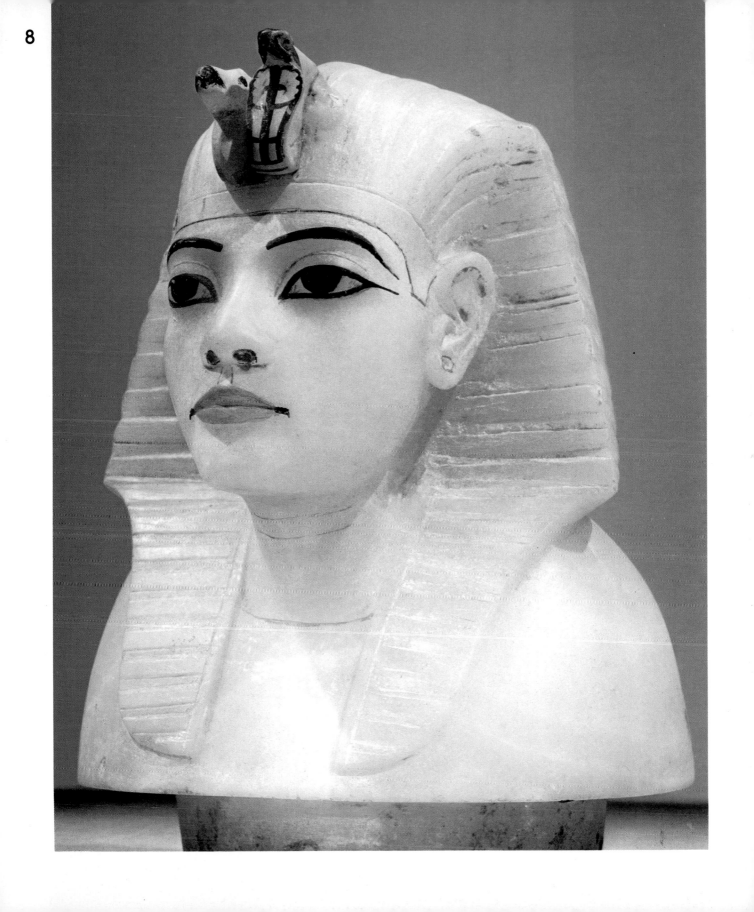

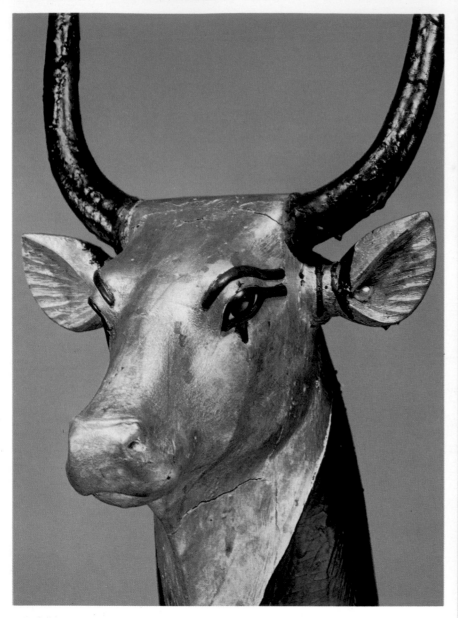

12

13

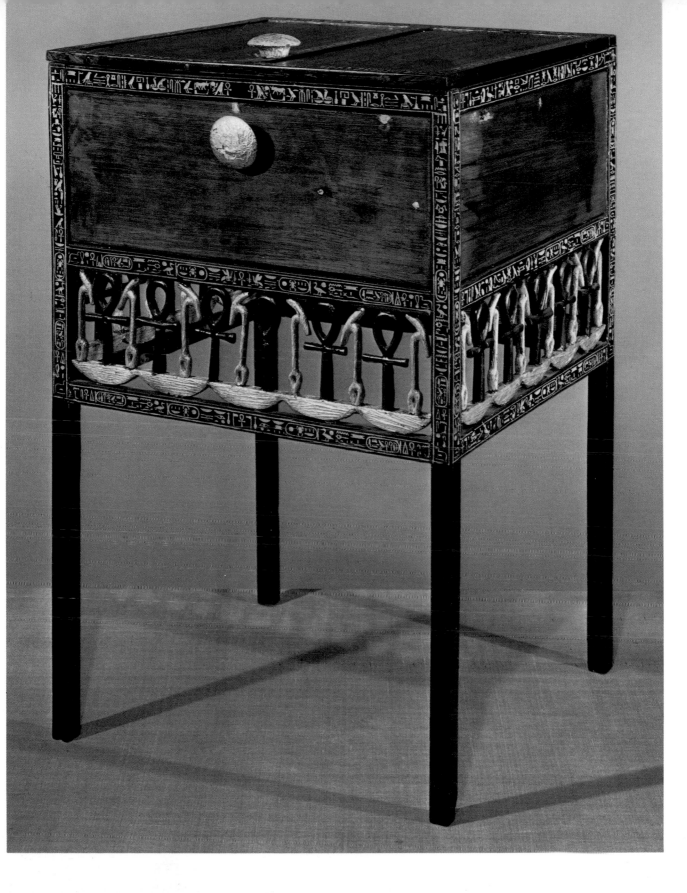

15

**18**

**20**

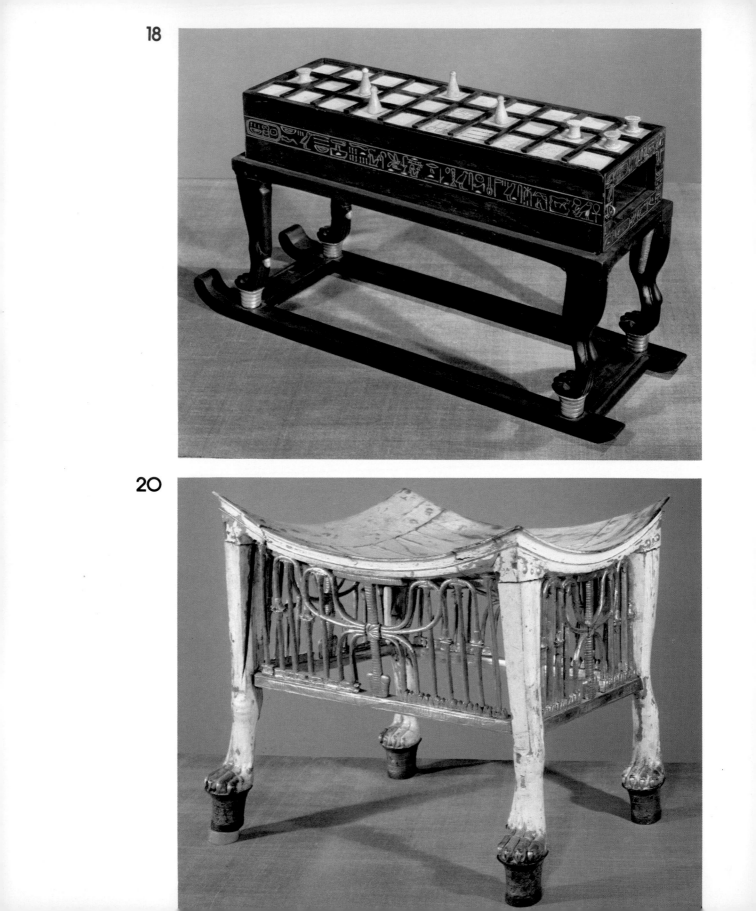

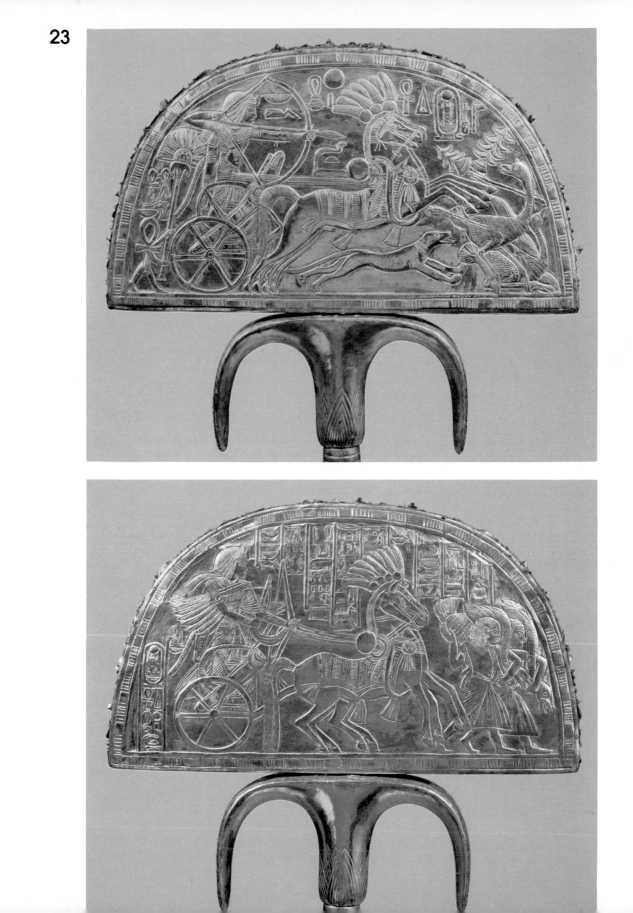

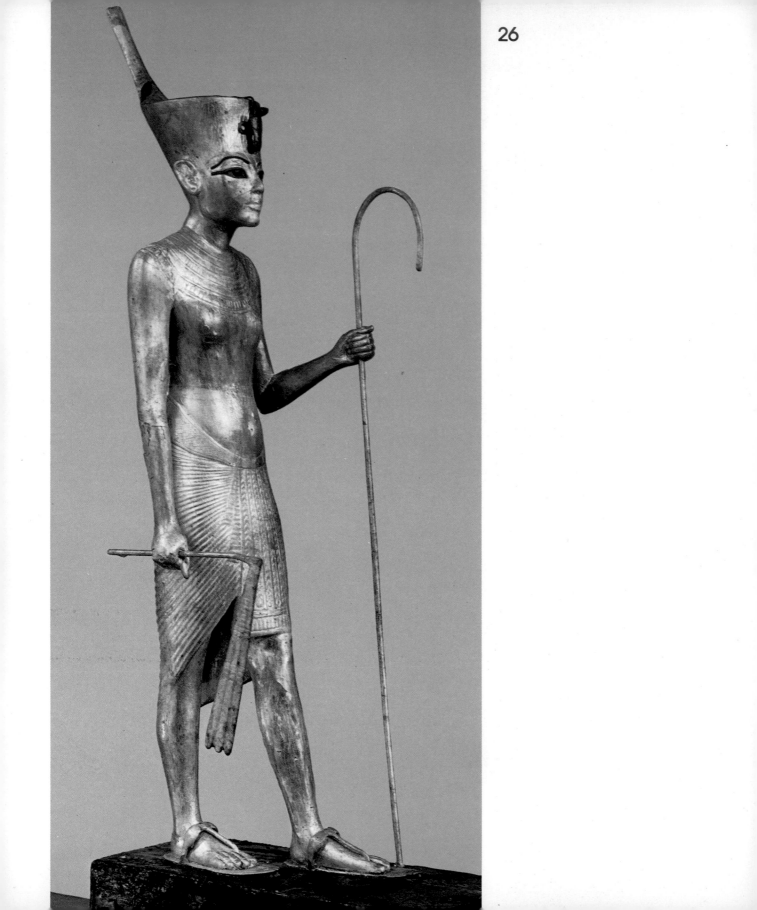

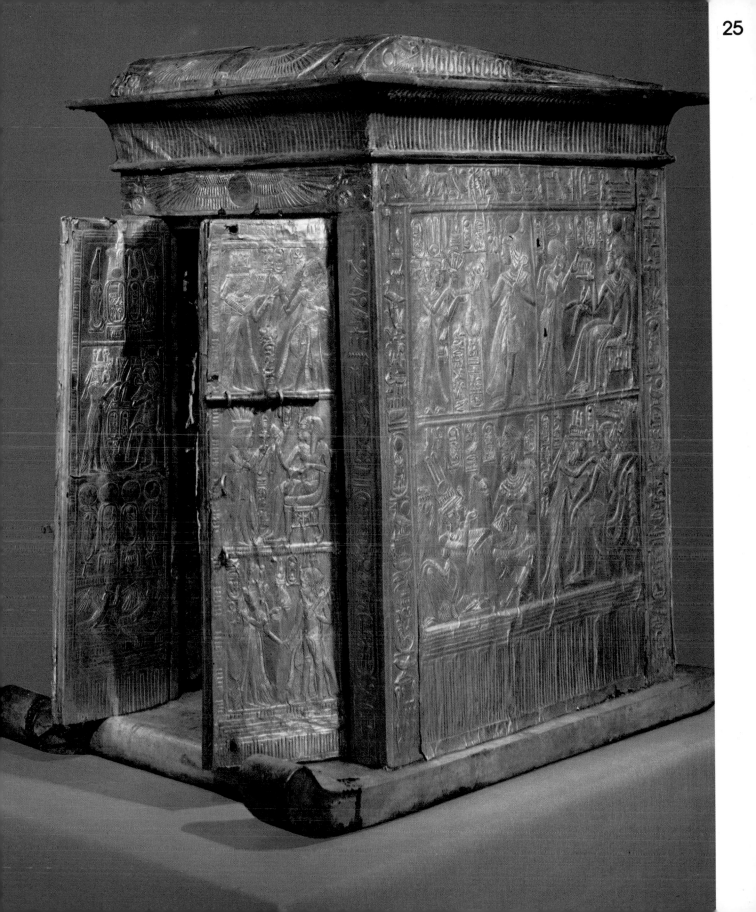

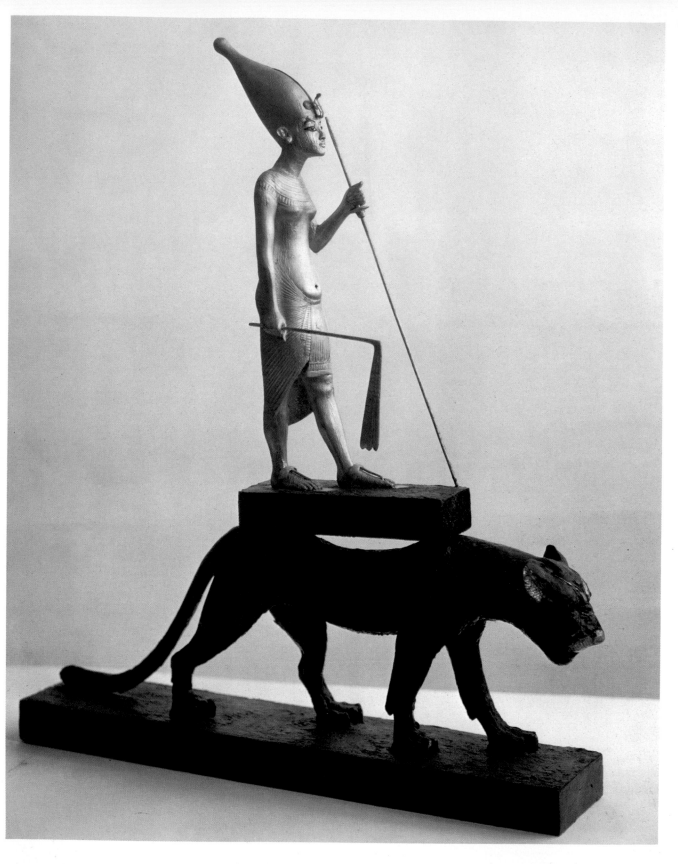

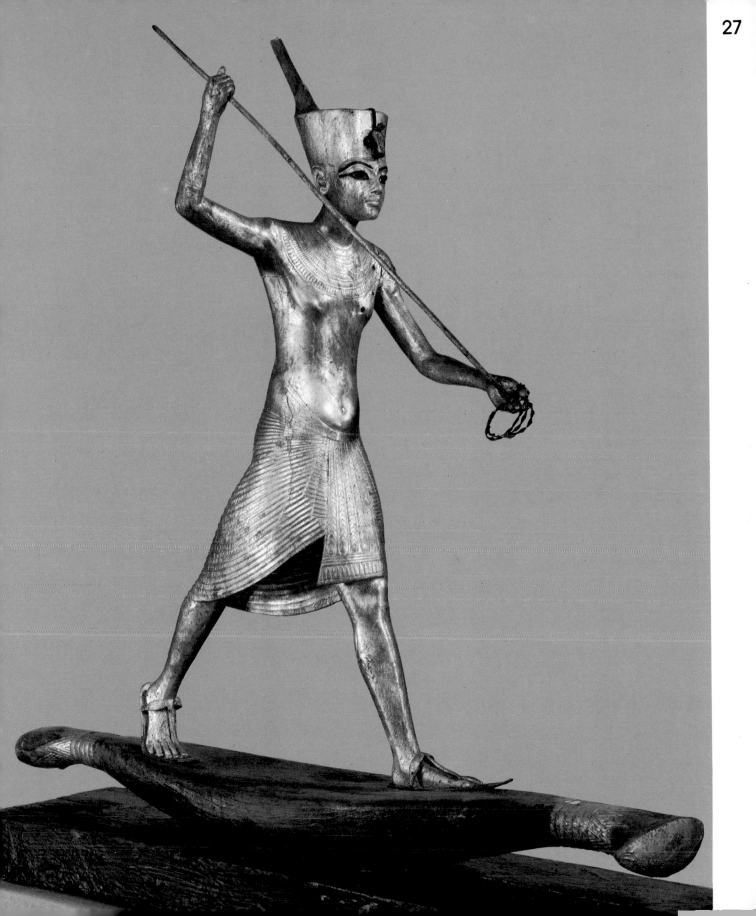

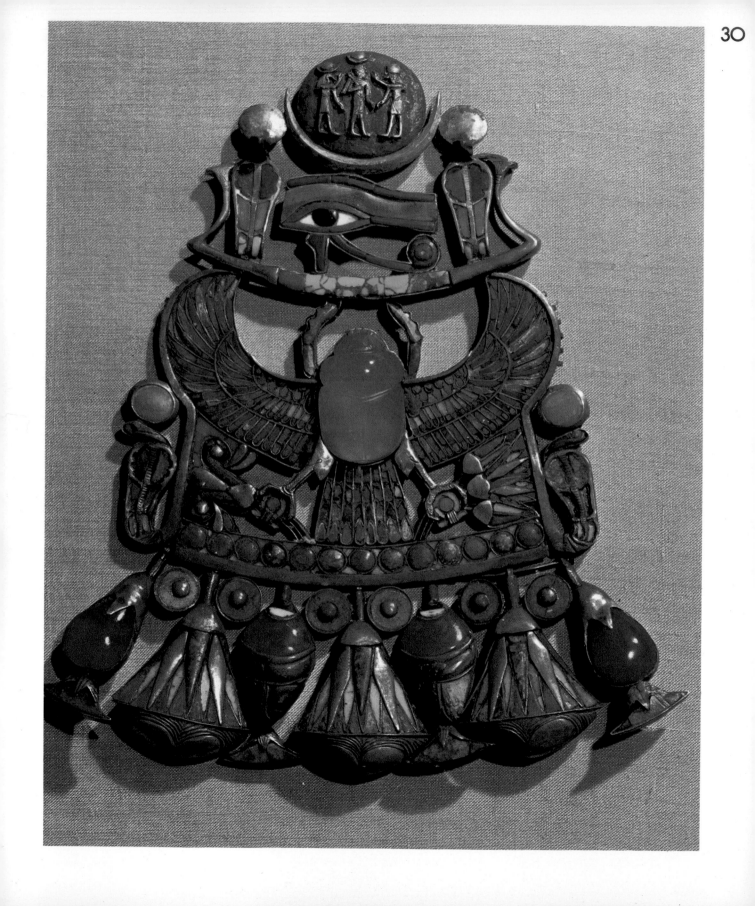

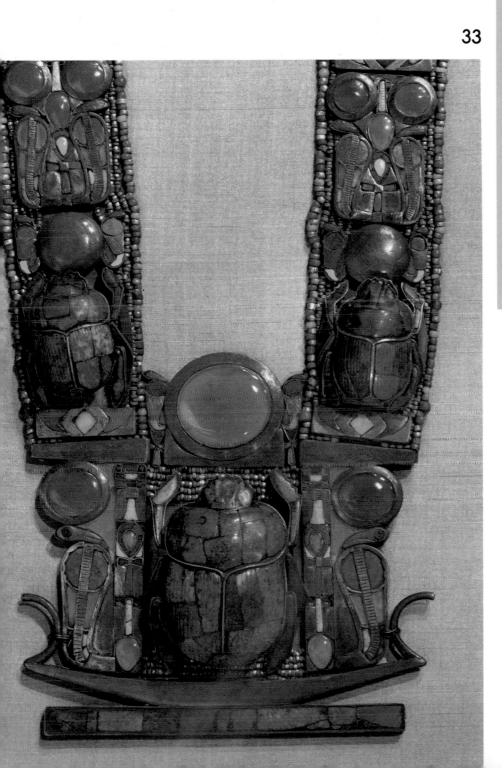

**33**

**35**

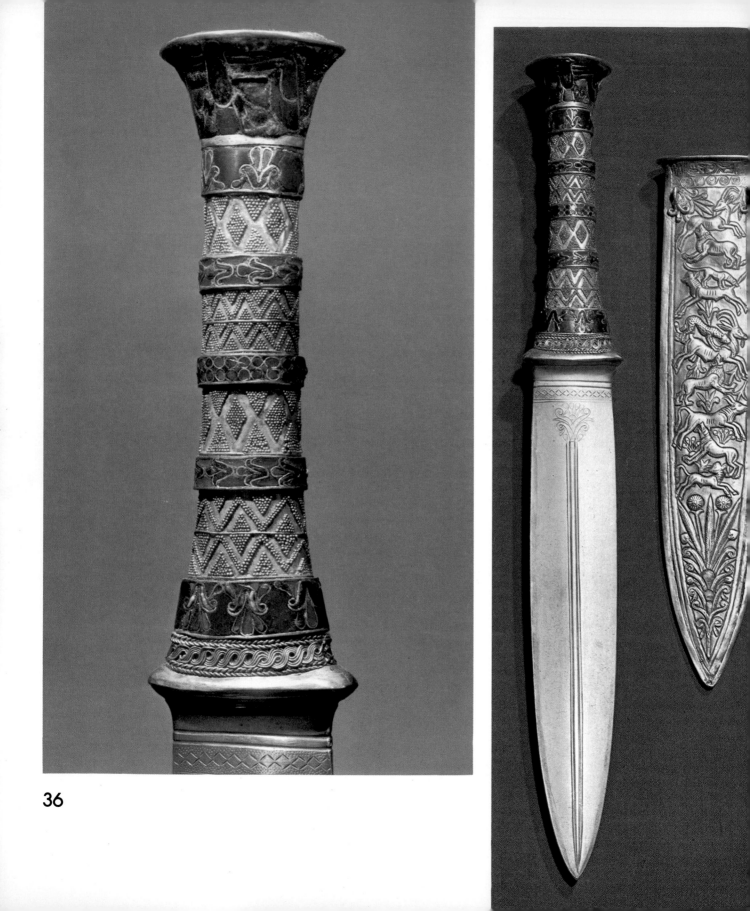

36

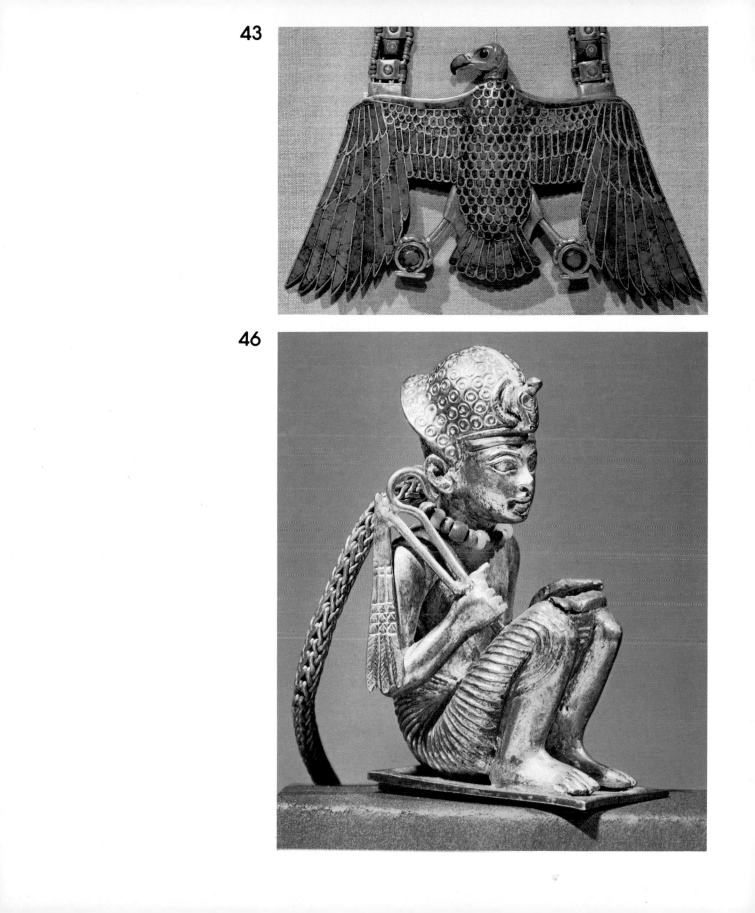

43

46

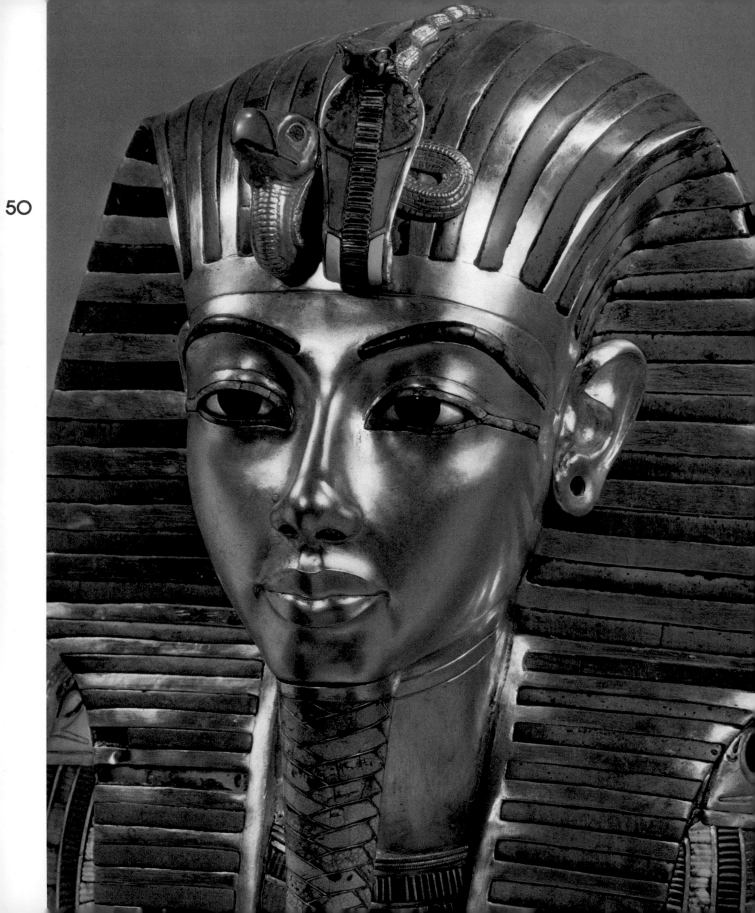

CATALOGUE

One of a pair of statues mounted on wooden pedestals and placed facing each other in the Antechamber, one on each side of the entrance to the Burial Chamber. It may truly be described as life-size because it corresponds very closely with the estimated height of the king, 1.676 metres (5 feet 6 inches), an estimate based on a measurement of his mummy. The king is represented in a conventional manner with the left leg forward, holding in his left hand a long staff, fitted with a handrest in the shape of a papyrus flower near the top, and in his right hand a mace. Both these objects, like the rest of his accoutrements, are gilded. The lobes of the ears are pierced (see no 39). On his head he wears the royal headcloth (*āfnet* meaning 'cover') with a long appendage at the back which is suggestive of the tail of a falcon. The head of the royal cobra inserted in the brow is made of bronze and overlaid with gold. The eyebrows, eyelids and kohl-marks extending sideways from the eyes are similarly made of gilded bronze. The white of the eye is made of crystalline limestone and the pupil of obsidian. Caruncles (small red patches) are shown on the inner and outer canthi of both eyes – a frequent mistake in Egyptian reproductions of the human eye which in nature shows a caruncle on the inner canthus only. Suspended from the neck, beneath a broad collar, is a shrine-shaped pectoral embodying a winged scarab – an amulet of a class frequently found on the chests of both mummies and statues (see nos 30 and 42). The rest of the gilded attire consists of a girdle with the king's name

on the buckle, a pleated kilt with animal heads in the lower corners, an apron decorated with a chevron design bordered by cobras with sun's disks on their heads, and two bracelets on each arm and wrist. On the feet are gilded bronze sandals.

The parts of the statue which are not gilded are coated with black resin painted directly on the wood, gesso being applied as an underlayer only to round off corners. Where it is gilded, pieces of linen were first glued to the wood, then a layer of gesso was spread over the linen and finally the overlay of gold was applied. Owing to the resin and the gold it is now impossible to see how many pieces of wood were used in its composition, but several joins are evident, including those of the ears, which were tongued to the head, the arms and the legs, which were rather crudely fixed to ill-fitting sockets by wedges. It will be noticed that the figure is not set square on the pedestal but is turned slightly to one side, so that it should be looking outwards when the side of the pedestal was placed against the wall. Its companion statue had a similar inclination.

In their position at the entrance to the Burial Chamber, these two statues gave the appearance of being sentinels, an impression heightened by the maces held in the outer hands. Perhaps this was a secondary function, although the mace by the time of Tutankhamun was no longer used as a weapon but only as a ceremonial implement. The inscription on the ornate panels of the apron reads: 'The Good God of whom one may be proud, the Sovereign of whom one boasts, the Royal Ka of (the)

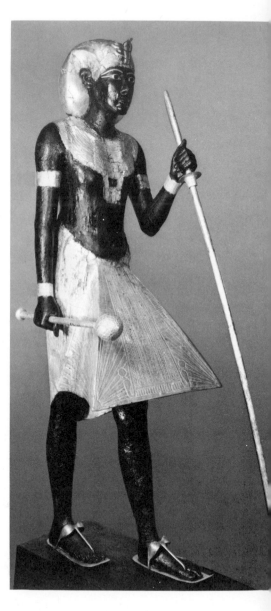

▷ Colour

Horakhty, (the) Osiris, King, Lord of the Two Lands, Nebkheperure' (*ie* Tutankhamun). After death, the king was thought to be identified both with the sun-god, of whom Horakhty was one appellation, and with Osiris, and consequently in this inscription the two names are virtually titles of the deceased Tutankhamun, whose spirit (*Ka*) was thus provided with a body, in the shape of each statue, which it could occupy. Black was the colour associated with regeneration, a conception which probably owes its origin to the black colour of the fertile soil of Egypt as a source of plant-life. The Egyptians called their country the Black Land (*Kemi*). Colour played an important part in magic and it seems evident that these statues were coated with black resin to increase their potency as instruments of regeneration. Mummies and coffins were sometimes coated with resin in the same way and doubtless for the same reason.

Apart from these two statues and a similar statue found in the tomb of Amenophis II (*c* 1450–1425 BC), the only other examples of their kind are three in this Museum, exhibited in the lobby at the northern end of the Sculpture Gallery. They were acquired in 1821 from the British Consul-General in Egypt, Henry Salt, who had obtained two of them from the tomb of Ramesses I (*c* 1320–1318 BC) at Thebes. The third may have come from the tomb of Ramesses II (*c* 1304–1237 BC) also at Thebes. Like those of Tutankhamun, these three statues were coated with black resin, which shows in some places impressions of the embossed patterns of the lost gilding. The discovery of the Tutankhamun examples has, for the first time, explained the function of the statues in the Museum's collection.

STATUE
Height 1.73 m, width 54.0 cm.
PEDESTAL
Height 17.0 cm, length 99.0 cm, width 34.0 cm.

Carter I: 99, pl XLI; II: 41; Desroches-Noblecourt 66, 265, 305, pls 32, LIII; Fox, pl 17; Lucas 98–100, 114; Vandier III: 355, 357–8; Paris Exh no 28.

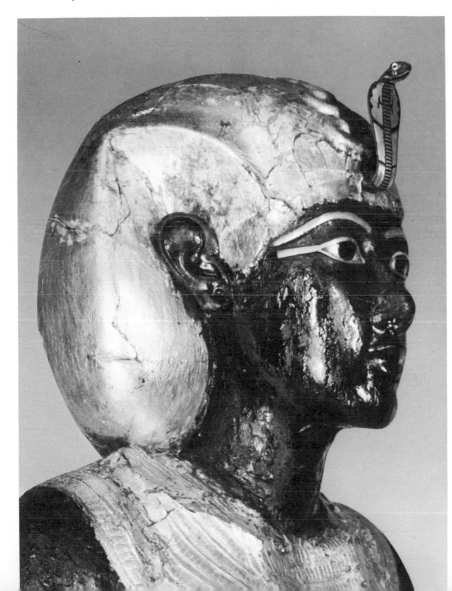

Apart from the yellow and green extensions with their shallow keēls at the stem and stern, the hull of this boat is carved from a single block of wood, probably acacia. It is shaped in a graceful curve to represent a carvel-built craft suitable for sailing on the Nile. The main deck has been hollowed to a depth of 1.5 centimetres below the level of the bulwarks. Amidships is an elongated cabin, its stepped roof following the curve of the hull and the walls of both its upper and its lower sections terminating at the top in coloured cavetto cornices. In the forecastle and the poop are screens for the crew, mounted on decks which overhang the gunwales on both sides. Two long steering paddles are manipulated in upright crutches held firmly at the top by a horizontal bar and fixed at the base to a cross-beam in front of the poop-deck. The walls of the screens and the cabin are covered with a multicoloured chequer pattern decoration broken on the port side of the cabin by four small windows in the upper section and two doors in the lower section. Two broad bands of the same decoration on the hull give the impression of strengthening ties. Painted on each side of the bows are a lotus flower, heads of the ram of Amun with uraeus and the falcon of Horus (on the port side with sun's disk, uraeus and two ostrich plumes), both mounted on pedestals, and a figure of the king as a sphinx wearing on his head the blue crown (*khepresh*) and trampling on a Nubian enemy. Above the sphinx is the sun's disk flanked by uraei. On the port side only is a

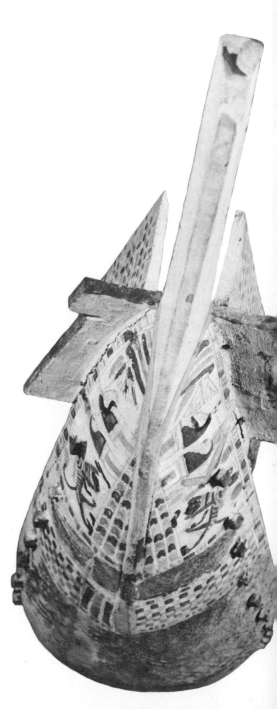

third pedestal supporting a winged falcon with the sun's disk and the sign for eternity between its wings. An empty cartouche is painted in front of the sphinx. In corresponding scenes on the stern are a figure of a winged goddess (Maāt) on a green basket (the emblem for universality) and three representations of the falcon-headed god of war, Mont, smiting Nubian and Asian enemies. The small rectangular projections on both sides of the upper part of the hull imitate the ends of thwarts inserted in carvel-built boats to yoke the two sides.

The boat was one of seven of its kind, which, together with four other boats equipped with masts, rigging and square sails, were stacked higgledy-piggledy, mostly on the tops of shrines, in the Treasury. Since it had neither oars nor sail it must have represented a barge which would be towed in a flotilla on some formal occasion. It may have been a model of one of the boats used to transport mourners and furniture to the tomb at the time of the king's funeral, or it may have been intended for his pilgrimage in the Afterlife to sacred places such as Abydos and Buto. Nothing in its build or decoration, which has several parallels on boats of the period, is truly indicative of its function.

Length 1.26 m, beam 22.0 cm, height 21.0 cm.

Carter III: 56–7, 60–1 (*cf* pls III and LXIIIB, which show a similar boat); Desroches-Noblecourt 83; Paris Exh no 29.

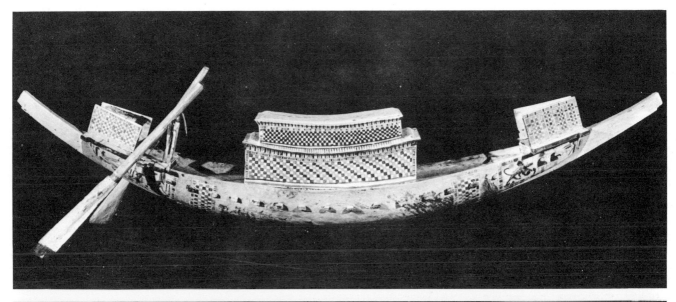

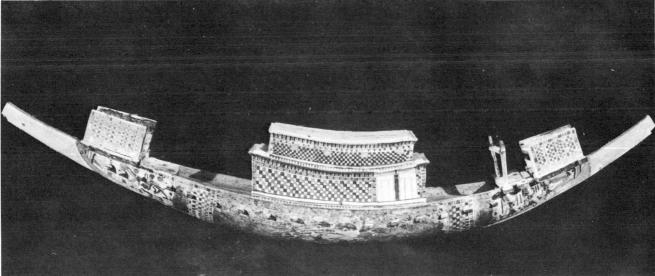

Floral motifs, particularly representations of the papyrus and the lotus, were often used to decorate Egyptian unguent vessels. The lotus was perhaps the most fragrant flower in the Nile Valley and therefore very appropriate for adorning containers intended for sweet-smelling unguents. The papyrus, however, was almost odourless and its association with the lotus in this connection is probably the result of the regular juxtaposition of the two plants in sculpture and painting as the respective emblems of Lower Egypt (papyrus) and Upper Egypt (lotus). With their stems intertwined they symbolized the union of the two divisions of the land at the beginning of the First Dynasty.

Carved of two blocks of alabaster of unequal height cemented together, this piece consists of a long-necked amphora and its stand, each flanked by symbols arranged symmetrically in an openwork design. On a level with the base of the vase and on the base of the vase itself is a double row of triangular incisions indicating a papyrus swamp. At each end of the row is a figure of a tadpole mounted on a ring of rope. As a hieroglyphic sign the tadpole means 'one hundred thousand' and the ring of rope 'eternity'. Grouped in this fashion the two signs convey the meaning 'one hundred thousand times eternity'. The notched stems above this group, which form the outermost elements in the handles of the vase, represent palm-ribs, the hieroglyphic sign for 'year'. Between the palm-ribs and the vase are the stems and flowers of papyrus and lotus, either growing from the swamp or tied to the neck of the vase by the so-called magical knot. On the front of the neck, carved in relief, is the head of the goddess Hathor; attached to her collar, which is incised and filled with a black pigment, is a lotus flower flanked by two buds and beneath it a single mandrake fruit. On the belly of the vase, under a frieze of petals, are representations of two human breasts and the names and titles of Tutankhamun, in part written defectively.

The stand consists of a central support flanked by two signs of 'life' (*ānkh*), the cross-pieces of which are in the form of human arms and hands, each holding the hieroglyph for 'welfare, prosperity' (*was*). The inner hands also hold single papyrus flowers and stems which extend from the inner *was* signs to the central support.

Some fifty alabaster (calcite) vases for unguents were found in the tomb, nearly all of them emptied of their contents by the robbers in their second visitation. It has been estimated that the total quantity of unguent placed in the tomb amounted to about 400 litres. That the robbers should have risked their lives to obtain it and also that they should have chosen it in preference to the many other treasures at their mercy would alone prove that it was a costly commodity. The vases being heavy and, in the case of this vessel and four others of the same general character, too large to move through the tunnel, the robbers poured the precious oils into water-skins for removal. Chemical analysis of the contents of one of the vessels found intact showed that the principal constituent was animal fat, to which some resin or balsam had been added, while cedar oil was identified as the base ingredient of another specimen. The perfume was extracted from flowers, gum-resins and other fragrant substances by wringing them in cloths and squeezing out the odoriferous liquids.

Height 50.0 cm, width 32.0 cm.

Carter I: pl XXII; Fox pl 13; Paris Ex no 36.

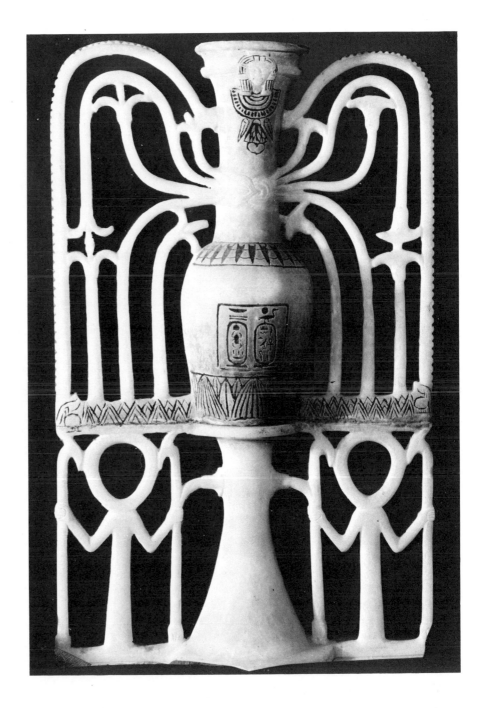

This alabaster unguent jar is carved in the form of a lion standing upright on a pedestal, the head and body being hollowed out to hold the unguent. The teeth and protruding tongue are made of ivory, the latter painted red. The left front paw rests on the hieroglyphic symbol for 'protection', while the right is held high. Both front paws have holes for the insertion of claws, perhaps of ivory. The right back paw, slightly raised, is placed in advance of the left, a pose which differs from that of standing figures of men in which the left leg is generally forward. Fixed to the top of the lion's head is a crownlike addition which serves as the mouth of the vase. It consists of a circular base from which project representations of pointed leaves of the blue lily and single lotus lilies surmounted by single papyrus flowers and small rosettes. Tufts of hair, inlaid with blue pigment, are engraved on the back of each shoulder (see no 37). The lobes of the ears are pierced to hold earrings. On the chest are inscribed the names and royal titles of Tutankhamun and

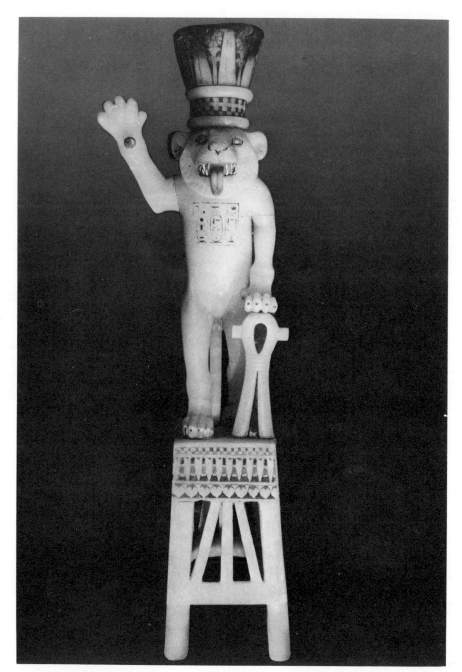

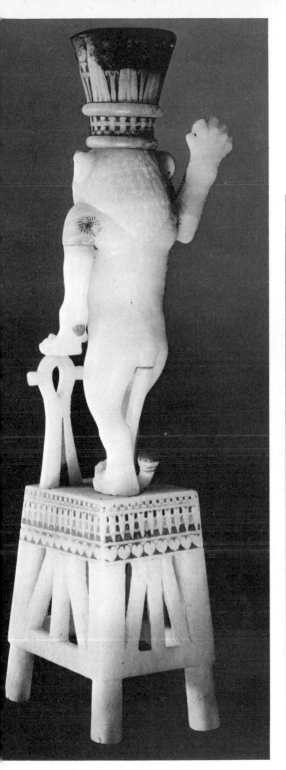

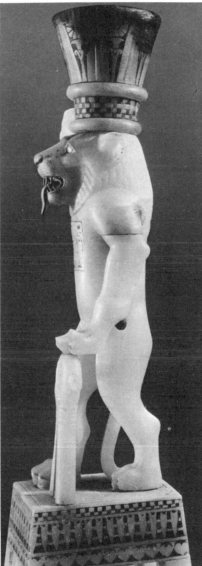

Ankhesenamun. Beneath the chequer pattern band of blue, black, white and yellow rectangles, the frieze of the pedestal consists of representations of individual lily petals and mandrakes.

Another alabaster unguent vase found in the tomb of Tutankhamun, but not included in this exhibition, is furnished with a lid on which is carved a lion closely resembling the lion of this vase, except that it is in a recumbent position. Two miniature lotus columns on the outside of the vase are surmounted by heads of the god Bes, a domestic deity associated with pleasures of every kind. Egyptian unguent vases frequently embodied in their composition a figure of Bes, usually represented as a bandy-legged dwarf with ears, mane and tail of a lion. The association between the god and, on the one hand, the lion and, on the other hand, unguent vases is thus very close and it seems evident that the lion-form was chosen for this vase because of the animal's connection with Bes and consequently with receptacles for unguents.

When found in the Annexe, it was in an upright position, but the crown had been wrenched off by the thieves and was lying on the floor nearby, its alabaster cover held in place by a linen binding. The dried fatty contents (see no 3), black in colour, remained intact.

Height 60.0 cm, width 19.8 cm.

Carter III: 144, 146, pl XLVIII; Desroches-Noblecourt 96; Riesterer pl 35; Paris Exh no 35.

The box and lid of this casket are carved each from a single piece of alabaster (calcite) and the two knobs are made of obsidian. The decoration throughout is incised and filled with coloured pigments. On the lid it consists of formal bouquets in which the chief components are a papyrus flower, cornflowers, mandrakes and lily petals. Two identical horizontal bands of blue lily petals beneath friezes of a chequer pattern decorate the box. At the head end the bands are broken by a rectangular frame within which are the cartouches of the king (left and centre) and of the queen (right). Above the cartouches are their titles 'Good God, Lord of the Two Lands' and 'Son of Re, Lord of Diadems' for the king, and 'Great Royal Wife' for the queen. The cartouches of the king are followed by the wish that he may be 'given life for ever and ever' and beneath the cartouche of the queen is the wish that she may 'be given life and be fruitful'.

When found, the casket was lying in the Antechamber with the lid removed, no doubt by the robbers. There was nothing to suggest that they had interfered with its contents, which consisted of a layer of cloth, a mass of decayed (horse?) hair and two balls of hair wrapped in linen, one 5 centimetres and the other 6 centimetres in diameter. Balls of dried Nile mud, sometimes with tufts of hair in the centre and sometimes with fragments of papyrus or linen, have been found in Egyptian tombs and they are thought to have had a magical significance, the nature of which is still obscure, although there is some evidence to suggest that they were asso-

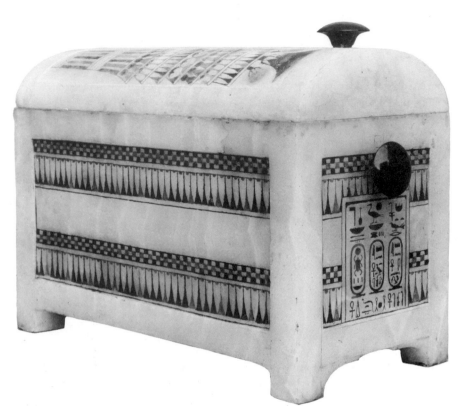

ciated with some form of contract. Since this casket bears the names of both the king and the queen, it is conceivable that each ball contains the hair of one of them. If some contract of importance was thereby signified, it may explain why such simple articles were placed in so elaborate a casket.

Length 33.0 cm, width 17.0 cm, height 24.0 cm.

Carter I: 200, pl LVIA; Keimer 145–57; USA Exh no 27; Japan Exh no 17.

This carved wooden figure of the anthropomorphic god Ptah is coated with gesso and gilded. Like many other objects found in the tomb of Tutankhamun, the gilt on the body is alloyed with copper, which gives it a reddish tinge, but on the face it seems to be unalloyed. The skull-cap is made of dark blue faience, and the eyes and eyebrows are inlaid with glass. A straight artificial beard of bronze incrusted with gold is represented as being held in position by sidestraps. As a rule figures of Ptah show the god wrapped in a shroud like a mummy, the head and hands alone being exposed, but in this figure the body is wrapped in a garment of feathers; a broad collar with back pendant (*mānkhet*) covers his chest and shoulders. In his hands he holds a sceptre (*was*) with animal head and the symbols for 'life' (*ānkh*) and 'stability' (*djed*). The figure is mounted on a pedestal of the same shape as the hieroglyphic sign for 'truth' (*maāt*) varnished with black resin and bearing in yellow paint the inscription: 'The Good God, Nebkheperure, Son of Re, Tutankhamun, ruler of southern On, beloved of Ptah, lord of truth, given life for ever'.

Ptah was the principal god of Memphis, the capital of Egypt in the time of the kings who built the pyramids, and his importance in the country as a whole must have been partly a result of his association with the early seat of government. In later times Amon-Re, the god of Thebes, achieved very wide recognition in a very similar way when Thebes was the capital. The Greeks identified Ptah with their god Hephaistus because he was the patron deity of artists

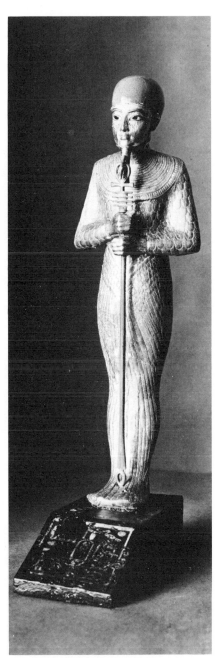

and craftsmen; his high priest bore the title 'Chief Artificer of Ptah'. An important inscription in this Museum, known as the Shabaka Stone, preserves a copy of the text of an ancient papyrus which claimed that Ptah was the universal creator; it was he who conceived the notion of mankind and all other living beings, and it was his word which brought them into existence. Other gods were immanent in him, merely members of his body, Atum, for example, being only the heart and tongue of Ptah.

FIGURE
Height 52.8 cm.
PEDESTAL
Length 26.0 cm, width 11.6 cm, height 7.4 cm.

Carter III: 52–3, pl LVB.

Carved of a single piece of alabaster (calcite) and inlaid with blue pigment, this chalice represents a single bloom of the white lotus (*Nymphaea lotus*), the characteristics of which, apart from its colour, are sixteen to twenty ovoid petals and four ovoid sepals. In this piece sixteen petals are shown, all carved in very delicate shallow relief. Rising from the base are two supports for the handles, each support consisting of a single flower of the blue lily (*Nymphaea caerulea*) and two buds. The petals and sepals of the blue lilies are narrow and pointed, and the number of petals in the flower is no more than twelve to sixteen. The handles, which are attached to the flowers and to the sides of the chalice, are composed of figures of Ḥeḥ, the god of eternity, kneeling on the emblem of universality and holding in each hand a palm-rib (the hieroglyphic sign for 'year', see no 3) and the sign for 'life' (*ānkh*).

Two inscriptions testify that Tutankhamun was the owner of the chalice. In the frame on the front are his prenomen and nomen with the appropriate titles and the epithet 'beloved of Amon-Re, lord of the Thrones of the Two Lands and lord of heaven, given life for ever'. On the lip of the chalice the band of inscription is divided into two, one reading to the right from the centre of the front and the other to the left:

To the right: 'May (he) live, the Horus Mighty Bull, beautiful of birth, the Two Ladies Goodly of Laws, who pacifies the Two Lands, the Horus of Gold Exalted of Crowns, who placates the gods, King of Upper and Lower Egypt and Lord of the Two Lands Nebkheperure, given life'.
To the left: 'May thy Ka live and mayest thou spend millions of years, thou who lovest Thebes, sitting with thy face to the north wind, thy two eyes beholding happiness'.

The chalice was found just inside the door of the tomb, whither it had been taken by the robbers, probably from the Annexe. Its discoverers called it the 'wishing-cup', from the wish at the end of the inscription. Cups and chalices in the form of the flower of a lily and dating from the Eighteenth–Twenty-second Dynasties are not uncommon; a small faience plaque in the Eton College collection actually shows Tutankhamun in the act of drinking from a large lotus chalice comparable in size with the present piece, but without handles. From the evidence at present available, it appears that the cups which represent the white lotus were used as drinking vessels, whereas those which represent the blue lily were used only for ritualistic purposes.

Height 18.3 cm, width 28.3 cm.
Depth of cup 16.8 cm.

Carter I: 110, 190, pl XLVI; Desroches-Noblecourt 64, 299, pl XXIIb; Fox pl 3; Tait 97; Paris Exh no 42.

▷ Colour

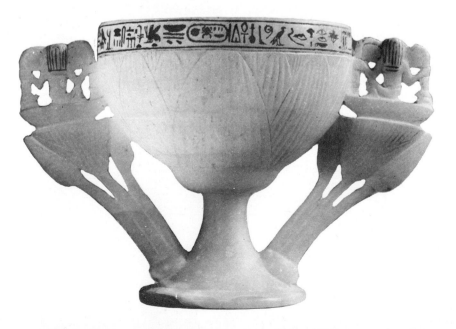

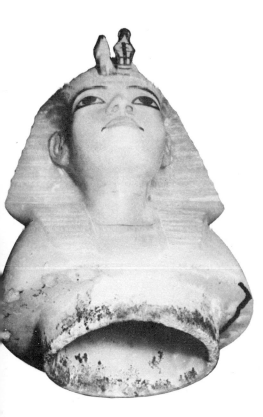

The gold miniature coffin (no 9) containing one of the king's internal organs, perhaps the lungs, was placed in one of four cylindrical compartments in a magnificent Canopic chest shaped like a shrine. The whole chest, except the movable lid, was carved of a single block of alabaster. On the outer walls were inscribed magical utterances by four goddesses, depicted at the four corners with their arms out-stretched, namely Isis, Nephthys, Selqet and Neith. They were the protectors of the Four Sons of Horus (Imset, Ḥapi, Qebḥsenuf and Duamutef), with whom the internal organs were identified. At the top of each of the inner compartments was a stopper, made of alabaster, in the form of the head and shoulders of a king wearing the striped royal headdress with the vulture's head and the cobra separately carved and inserted in the brow. Details of the features are picked out in black and red. The likeness to Tutankhamun is so striking that it is hard to imagine the sculptor was not portraying the king himself.

Although chests which contained the deceased's mummified viscera are known as Canopic chests, the name has no historical justification. Usually such chests held four jars, the actual receptacles of the viscera, which, until shortly after the time of Tutankhamun, were provided with human-headed stoppers. Later, one stopper only was human-headed and three represented heads of a baboon, a jackal and a falcon, the forms ascribed to the Four Sons of Horus. Canopus was the name given by the Greeks to a town near Alexandria after one of their legendary heroes, Canopus, the pilot of Menelaus, perhaps because they believed he was buried there. It was the seat of a cult of Osiris in which the god was represented as a bulbous jar with a human head, not unlike the jars used for preserving the viscera. Once the town had acquired its name, it is not difficult to understand how ancient visitors to Egypt imagined that it was Canopus himself, and not Osiris, who was worshipped in the form of a human-headed jar. Early European antiquarians, unaware of the difference between the Osiris-jars and the human-headed jars which contained the viscera, added to the error of the ancients by associating the viscera-jars with Canopus and calling them Canopic jars, a name which they have retained to this day.

Tutankhamun's Canopic chest, covered by a linen pall, was placed on a gilded wooden sledge against the east wall of the Treasury. It was enclosed in a wooden shrine with a cavetto cornice surmounted by a frieze of cobras, the whole overlaid with gold. Above the shrine was a golden canopy supported at the corners by posts which rested on the sledge. Gilded wooden figures of the goddesses Isis, Nephthys, Neith and Selqet, with arms stretched sideways and facing the four walls of the shrine, were also mounted on the sledge. Mistakes had been made by those who assembled the Canopic equipment in antiquity, both in the placing of two of the figures of the goddesses and in the arrangement of two of the miniature coffins.

Height 24.0 cm, maximum depth 19.0 cm.

Carter III; 46, 48–50, pls V, IX, X and LIIIB; Desroches-Noblecourt 78, 83, 222, 238, 246, 301, pls 133, XXXIII; Aldred 87, pl 152; Fox 27, pls 44–5; Paris Exh no 30; USA Exh no 24; Japan Exh no 15.

▷ Colour

One of four miniature coffins, all of the same form but differing in their inscriptions, which were placed in an alabaster chest (see no 8), the so-called Canopic chest. They are made of beaten gold, inlaid with coloured glass and carnelian. Each coffin contained one of the internal organs of the king – liver, stomach (or spleen), lungs and intestines – which were removed from his body during the process of embalming. In design these coffins are miniature replicas of the second of the three anthropoid coffins within which the king's mummy was placed.

Tutankhamun's names in the inscriptions appear to have been substituted for others which have been completely erased. It may therefore be conjectured that the coffins, like some of the other objects in the tomb, were originally made for Smenkhkare. This explanation would account for the general facial resemblance to Tutankhamun if, as seems probable, the two kings were brothers.

The mummiform effigy is portrayed wearing the striped royal headdress (nemes), with the vulture's head and the cobra on the brow, a plaited beard on the chin and an elaborate collar composed of imitations of petals. The lobes of the ears are pierced for earrings after the fashion of the period. Crossed over the chest and held in each hand are the shepherd's crook and the flail, emblems of the god Osiris with whom the dead king was identified. Two vultures, one with the head of a cobra representing the goddess Wadjet and the other representing the goddess Nekhbet, spread their wings over the

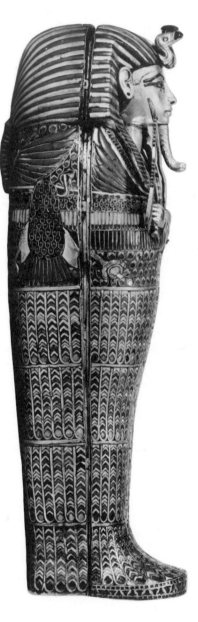

arms and shoulders of the effigy; they hold in their claws the hieroglyphic sign for 'eternity' (shen). The lower part of the body is decorated in cloisonné work with a stylized feather pattern arranged in compartments. In the centre of the front, inlaid in coloured glass, is the inscription, 'Words spoken by Nephthys: "I embrace with my arms that which is in me, I protect Hapy who is in me, Hapy of the Osiris, King Nebkheperure [ie Tutankhamun], justified before the great god"'. The goddess Nephthys, on the underside of the lid, is shown standing on the hieroglyphic sign for 'gold' (nub) and enveloping with her wings a packet containing one of the internal organs, perhaps the lungs. The remainder of the inside of the lid and the whole of the inside of the box are covered with magical inscriptions. (See also the description of no 8.)

Length 39.5 cm, width 11.5 cm, height 12.5 cm.

Carter III: 46–51, pls LIII and LIV; Desroches-Noblecourt 83, 220, 222, 301, pl XXXIV; Fox pl 46; Piankoff, 19, pl 9; Paris Exh no 31; USA Exh no 2; Japan Exh no 2.

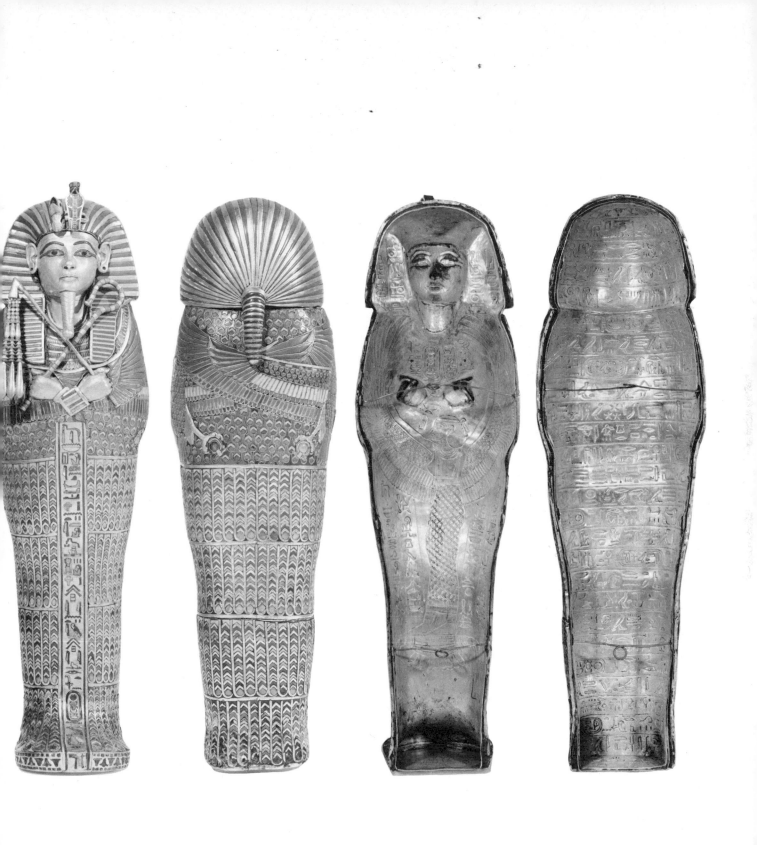

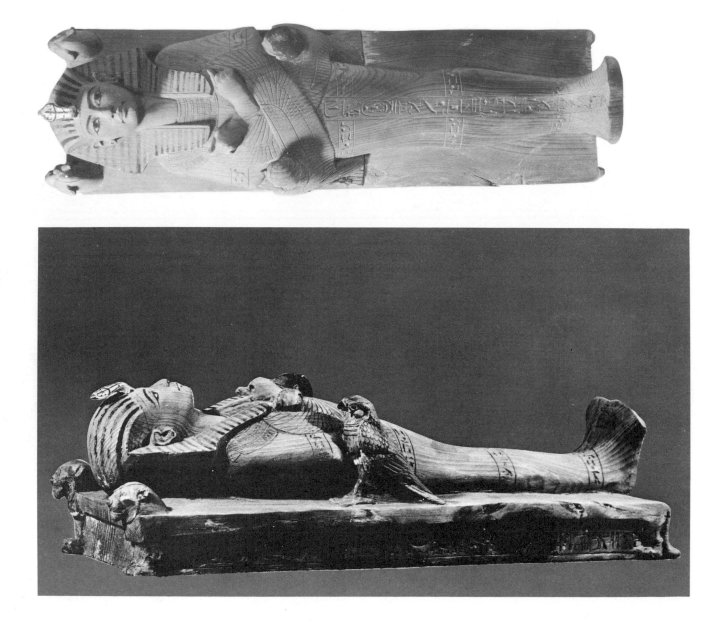

Carved from a single piece of wood, this model consists of a figure of the king, his body wrapped in a shroud, lying on a bier in the form of two lions with elongated bodies. Apart from the hands, which once held the crook and flail (the insignia of Osiris), nothing can be seen of the king's body except the head and neck on which the royal *nemes* headdress is placed. At the sides of the body, immediately beneath the elbows, are carved, almost in the round, small figures of a falcon and a human-headed bird (Ba), each with one wing laid on the body of the king. It was a gift by a high official named Maya.

Like so many other objects from the tomb of Tutankhamun, this piece has no parallel. It was placed in a small rectangular wooden sarcophagus and in this respect, as well as in its general appearance, it is reminiscent of some of the Ushabti figures of its period. Moreover, Maya also gave one of the Ushabtis found in this tomb. Its purpose, however, was quite different. The twin lion-bed on which the figure lies resembles both the bed used by the embalmers when mummifying the body and the so-called funerary bed on which it was taken to the tomb. Tutankhamun's funerary bed, which was found beneath his outermost coffin, was made of gilded wood and its design was very similar to the pattern of this model. Everything seems to show that the piece represents in miniature the body of the king lying on his funerary bed after the completion of the process of mummification. The wrappings and enveloping shroud, which were held in position by

one vertical and four horizontal bandages, are indicated in this piece by bands of inscription. The human-headed bird and the falcon are two of the forms which the disembodied king might adopt when visiting his body after it was mummified. A high Egyptian official who lived not long before the time of Tutankhamun included in his tomb at Elkab an inscription containing a promise by the gods to grant him the power to transform himself into 'a phoenix, a swallow, a falcon or a heron', transformations of a kind which are also mentioned in the Book of the Dead (*cf* chapters 77–8, 83–6). Another chapter (no 89) has, as its vignette, a representation of the human-headed bird hovering over the body of the deceased which lies on a funerary bed of the same kind as this piece.

The inscription on the central bandage reads: 'Words recited by King Nebkheperure [*ie* Tutankhamun]: "Descend, my mother Nut, spread thyself over me and let me be the Imperishable Stars that are in thee." '

The inscriptions on the bier record that the object was the gift of the Superintendent of Building Works in the Necropolis, Royal Scribe and Superintendent of the Treasury, Maya.

Like many of the Ushabti figures, this model was found in the room called by the excavators the Treasury.

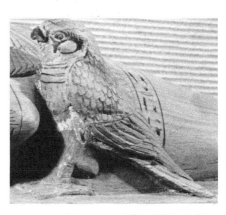

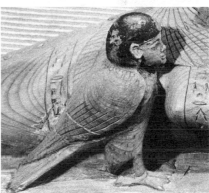

Length 42.2 cm, width 12.0 cm.
Height of bier 4.0 cm.

Carter III: 84–6, pl XXIV; Desroches-Noblecourt 216–9, pls 182, LIV; Fox pl 55; Schulman 66–8; Zabkar 84; Paris Exh no 34.

▷ Colour

As a rule Ushabti figures, even those of kings, were merely formal representations, not portraits. In this case the sculptor has produced in wood (cedar?) what appears to be a likeness of Tutankhamun, the lower part of the body being shrouded like a mummy. On his head he wears the blue striped *nemes* headdress – a royal accoutrement – and on his brow is the uraeus. A soul-bird (see no 10) is placed on his chest, its wings, like the bead collar above it, extending from one shoulder to the other. In his hands are the emblems of the god Osiris, a crook and a flail, instead of the agricultural implements normally carried by non-royal persons. The inscription on the front of the figure is a version of chapter 6 of the Book of the Dead. An inscription written in hieratic on one of the boxes which contained Tutankhamun's Ushabtis records that the figures were made of *mry* wood to which gold leaf had been applied, but the wood has not yet been identified.

Ushabti figures are among the commonest objects which have been preserved from ancient Egypt. Some 413 figures of varying quality and material were found in this tomb alone, and the tomb of Sethos I, who reigned about thirty-five years later than Tutankhamun, yielded about 700, by far the highest total from any single tomb. When Ushabtis were first introduced as part of the equipment of an Egyptian tomb (under the Eleventh–Twelfth Dynasties, *c* 2000 BC), they were very few in number, sometimes only one figure in a tomb. Their number was not substantially augmented until the

Eighteenth Dynasty (*c* 1567–1320 BC). In the case of non-royal persons the ideal number – at least at certain times – was 401, one figure for every single day in the year and 36 foremen to control each group of ten figures. The figures were made in the temple workshops under the direction of a priest who bore the title 'Chief Fashioner of Amulets', no doubt because the main occupation of his workshop was the manufacture of the small protective amulets which were placed in the mummy-wrappings and were worn by persons in life. The family of a dead person bought the figures and the money paid served the dual purpose of paying the vendor and paying the notional wages of the figures.

Although they were sometimes called 'servants' in the Egyptian texts, Ushabtis were more often considered as substitutes or deputies for their deceased owner when he was required by the god Osiris to perform corvée duties of an agricultural kind in the Next World. This conception underlies the spell from the Book of the Dead (chapter 6) which is inscribed on the front of this figure. The dead Tutankhamun is represented as addressing the Ushabti and instructing him that if he (*ie* Tutankhamun) is summoned to work in the god's domain 'to cultivate the fields, to irrigate the riverbanks or to transport the sand of the east to the west' he (*ie* the Ushabti) shall say that he is ready to do the work for him. The text finishes with the statement that Tutankhamun is in the company of the god Ptah-Seker-Osiris, lord of the

necropolis, living and prosperous for ever.

Incised under the feet is the inscription: 'Made by the Royal Scribe and General of the Army, Minnakht, for his lord, the Osiris king Nebkheperure, justified'. The figure was therefore a gift from the general to the king's funerary equipment.

Height 52.0 cm, width 16.5 cm.

Carter III: 82–4; Desroches-Noblecourt fig 163; Černý 12–13; Schulman 61–66 and 68; USA Exh no 17.

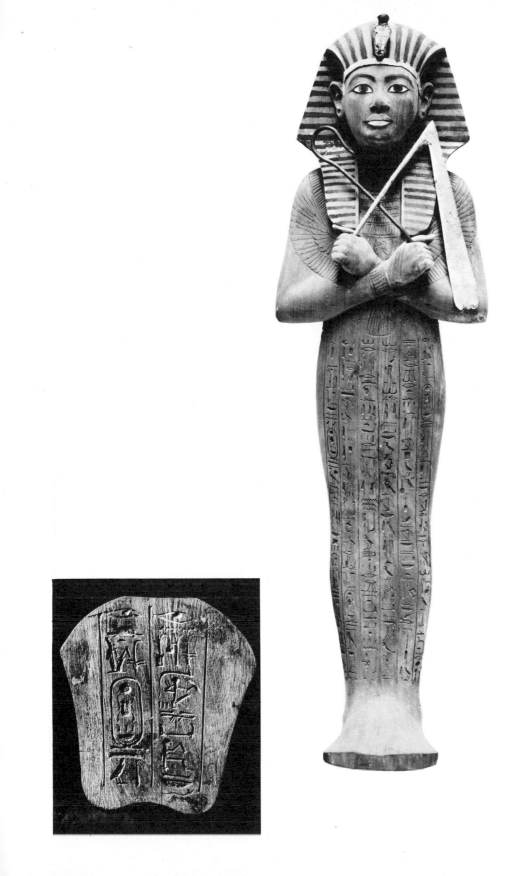
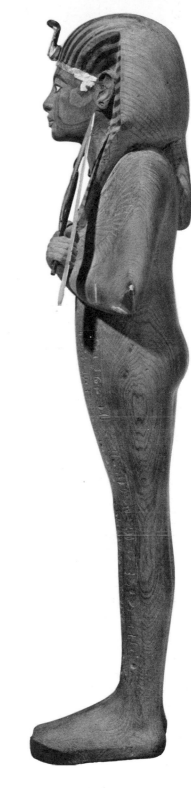

Carved from a block of wood, this head
was first covered with a thin layer of
gesso and then gilded. In the lower part of
the neck the gesso is coated with black
varnish. The horns, also made of wood,
are overlaid with a thin sheet of copper or
bronze and varnished black. The eyebrows and eyelids are represented in black
glass inlay, the eyeballs probably in
white glass and the pupils either in black
glass or in obsidian. It is attached to a
wooden stand varnished with black resin.
Traces of decoration under the varnish
seem to be detectable.

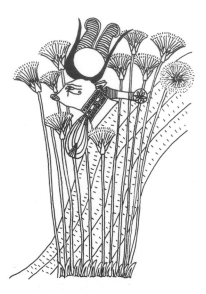

As a sacred animal the cow was
especially associated with Hathor, one of
whose functions was to serve as the local
goddess of the Theban necropolis. She
had an important sanctuary in Deir
el-Bahri at the foot of the western
mountain of Thebes. She is often
represented as a cow standing with her
back to the mountain, parting with her
head the stems of papyrus which grow at
her feet. Only the head is visible, the rest of
the body being concealed by the papyrus.
In every probability this gilded head was
intended to represent Hathor in her
capacity as the tutelary deity of the
necropolis in which the tomb of
Tutankhamun was located. It is, however,
not common for a deity or a sacred
animal to be shown incomplete, although
there are exceptions (see no 2). Hathor,
in particular, did not conform with the
normal pattern, her face alone being
represented regularly on the capitals of
architectural columns and on the handles
of sistra. Although the gilding of the face

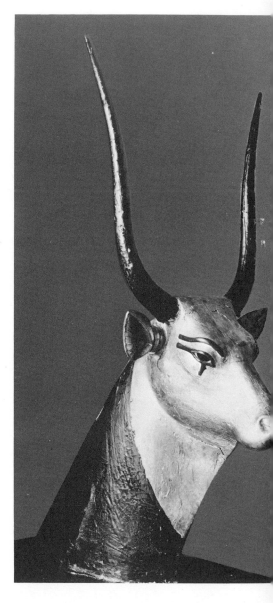

in this piece may not be intended to bear
any special significance, it is worth noting
that gold was thought to be connected
with Hathor, one of whose epithets was
'the golden'.

This head, partly enveloped in a linen
cloth knotted at the throat, was found in
the Treasury near the doorway.

Height 91.6 cm.

Carter III: 33, 46, pls IVB, LIXA;
Desroches-Noblecourt 250, pl XLVIII;
Fox pl 41.

▷ Colour

Made of wood coated with gesso and gilded, this bed consists of four detachable members: two sides in the form of long slender cows with lyriform horns and sun's disks, an imitation string-mesh mattress to which the footboard is joined by curved braces, and a hollow rectangular pedestal. The feet of the animals fit into sockets in the pedestal and the frame of the mattress is attached by wooden hooks at the ends of the cross bars to metal staples on the inner flanks of the animals. By this method of construction the beds could be taken apart for conveyance to the tomb and quickly reassembled. Two other beds found with this piece in the Antechamber, but not shown in the exhibition, represent lions or lionesses and composite animals with heads and necks which Carter described as half hippopotamus and half crocodile and leopard bodies. All three beds have slightly curved mattresses and the tails of the animals are curled upwards over the bodies.

In addition to these three beds, Tutankhamun's tomb furniture included four beds of a more conventional kind, three of them richly gilded and orna-mented, and a fifth bed of a folding kind like a camp-bed. Although it cannot be proved that the beds with theriomorphic sides were intended for special purposes, enough evidence exists to indicate unmistakably that they were not used by the king in his lifetime. Each bed is inscribed on the upper surface of the frame of the mattress at the head-end with a short dedicatory text, the most important elements of which are the name of the king

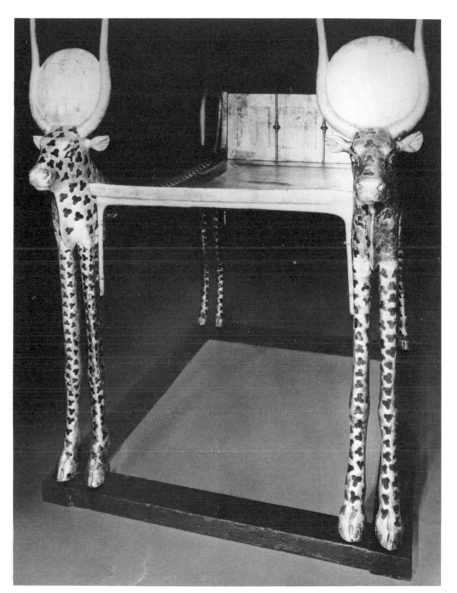

▷ Colour

followed by the formula 'true of voice' and
the words 'beloved of' a certain deity, the
whole inscription being written in a cartouche. On this bed the inscription reads:
'May the Good God live, may he be one
who lives for ever, (namely) the Lord of
the Two Lands who holds the sovereignty
of Re, the Osiris, king of Upper Egypt
Nebkheperure, true of voice, beloved of
Isis-Meḥt'. Both the title 'the Osiris' and
the formula 'true of voice' refer only to
dead persons and consequently the
funerary character of the bed is not in
doubt. Equally certain is the bovine nature
of the protecting deity, because in the
hieroglyphic writing her name is determined by a hybrid figure with the body of a
woman and the head of a cow surmounted
by horns and the sun's disk. Apart from
Hathor, the most important cow-goddess
in the Egyptian pantheon was Meḥturt
(a name meaning 'the great flood'), who
symbolized both the primordial waters
and the celestial ocean across which the
boat of the sun-god was believed to sail in
its daily journey from the eastern to the
western horizon. At an early date Meḥturt
became identified with Hathor and, since
Hathor was also identified with Isis, it
followed that Meḥturt and Isis were
associated. The name written Isis-Meḥt in
the inscription may be an abbreviation for
the fuller form Isis-Meḥturt, but such is
the nature of hieroglyphic writing that the
cow-headed determinative may have been
considered sufficient to show that the
actual reading was not Meḥt but Meḥturt.

Another explanation is, however,
possible. In the corresponding inscription

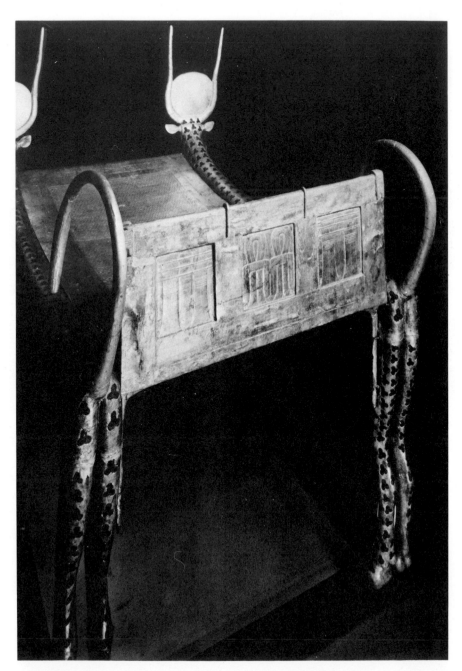

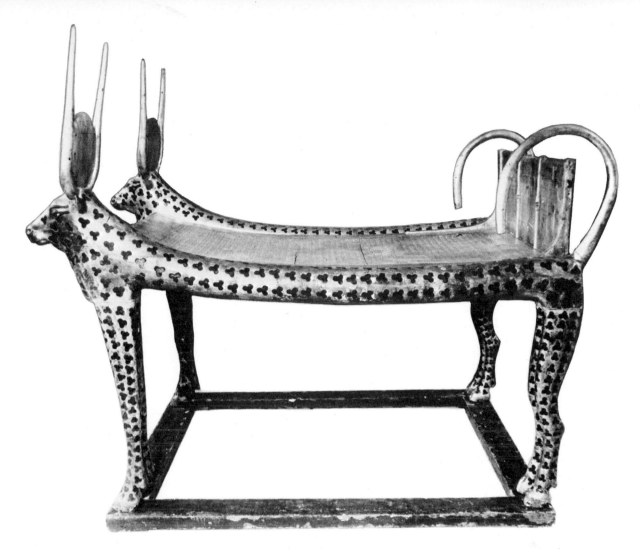

on the leonine bed the deity is, surprisingly, Meḥturt, the name being spelt fully and open to no doubt, though the determinative is damaged and the head of the goddess, presumably that of a lioness, is destroyed. But Meḥturt was not a lioness, whereas Meḥt (and Isis-Meḥt) was a leomorphic deity. In view of this irregularity it may be conjectured that the scribe, or the artist, was guilty of a confusion and the deity of the leonine bed should be Isis-Meḥt, while that of the cow-bed should be Meḥturt. In the case of the third bed the deity named is Ammut. In the judgment scenes depicted in the vignettes

of the Book of the Dead, a ferocious creature with the head of a crocodile, the forepart of the body of a leopard and the hindquarters of a hippopotamus is regularly represented waiting to devour the deceased if he should fail to pass the test when his heart is weighed in the balance against the feather of truth. This creature is always named Ammut 'Devourer of the Dead'. While it is true that in this bed the faces are those of hippopotami, the bodies are those of leopards and, at most, only the backs of the heads and the necks belong to crocodiles, the animals in the composition are

the same as those in the normal representations of Ammut. Perhaps one reason for the difference in the parts of the animals selected was that only the leopard could provide the physical form necessary for the slender sides and legs of the bed. Nevertheless it is strange to find a creature with the hostile attributes of Ammut chosen, it might seem gratuitously, for inclusion in the king's tomb equipment.

Although these three beds are the only three-dimensional examples of their kind at present known, similar beds are represented in the scenes carved and painted on a wall in the tomb of Ramesses

III (*c* 1198–1166 BC). Such scenes are always magical in character and were intended to provide the deceased owner of the tomb with what was considered necessary to reach the Next World and to lead his life there without risk of succumbing to the various dangers which were thought to beset his journeys with Re, the sun-god, across the sky and through the underworld. There can be no doubt that Tutankhamun's theriomorphic beds were also designed for magical purposes. In the cases of the leonine bed and the bed of Ammut, the nature of the purpose is still not clear (see no 10), but an ancient legend found in some of the royal tombs, and actually inscribed on one of the golden shrines which protected the mummy of Tutankhamun, explains the function of the cow-bed beyond any doubt. According to the legend, known as the *Destruction of Mankind*, Re, while he was still ruling on earth but having grown old, discovered that men were conspiring against him and he therefore resolved to destroy them. After consultation with the other gods he sent his eye in the form of the goddess Hathor to carry out his resolve. Before she had completed the massacre, however, Re relented and brought it to an end by a trick, which made the goddess drunk and incapable of further destruction. Nevertheless he was still angry with his disloyal subjects and decided to retire to heaven. The journey from earth to heaven was accomplished on the back of a cow-goddess whose body then became the sky itself. On the shrine of Tutankhamun the cow-goddess is called Nut, but references to the transportation in the Coffin Texts of the Middle Kingdom identify her with Meḥturt.

The ancient Egyptians were always concerned about the method whereby the passage from earth to heaven could be achieved. A thousand years and more before the time of Tutankhamun their kings built pyramids which were material representations of the sun's rays and, through the processes of magic, served as substitutes for the rays when the sun was not shedding its rays from heaven to earth. Through the possession of a pyramid the king could thus ascend to heaven whenever he chose to do so and could return to earth at will. By the time of Tutankhamun the custom of building pyramids had long been discontinued, but the need for some means of transportation remained. The cow-bed, in which the duplication of the animal figures was dictated by practical reasons, supplied the need and Tutankhamun no doubt imagined that when all his funerary rites had been performed he would be able to emulate the sun-god and ascend to heaven, reclining on his bed mounted on the back of Meḥturt.

The heads and bodies of both the cows are covered with trefoils of dark blue paste sunk in the gold. At the tip of the tail may be seen wavy red lines which represent hairs. On both faces of the footboard are three rectangular compartments, the outermost decorated with pairs of *djed* amulets symbolizing stability and the middle compartment with a pair of *tit* amulets known as the girdle of Isis which also signified welfare. Single papyrus flowers and stems are represented as if hanging from the crossrail and sprouting from the base of the panels between the compartments, probably because they were symbols of strength and vigour. Each of the curved braces, which join the footboard to the mattress, is ornamented with a ribbon decoration.

This bed was placed in the Antechamber between the other two beds.

COW FIGURES
Length 2.21 m, height 1.79 m.
PEDESTAL
Length 1.78 m, width 1.28 m.

Carter I: 98, 112–3, pl XVIII; Desroches-Noblecourt 265, pl XXIX; Baker 108, fig 145; Drioton 41, pl 109; Fox pl XII; Piankoff 26–37, pl 14; Riesterer 58–9, pls 22–3; Paris Exh no 27.

Both the gable lid and the box of this chest consist of ebony frameworks and recessed inner panels of red wood, probably cedar. The joints are either dovetailed or mortise and tenon, the latter being secured by wooden pegs. As a border to each panel there are three or four contiguous strips of ivory and polished ebony veneer laid alternately. At the top of the box, projecting outwards beyond the line of the lid, is a plain cavetto cornice with a gilded moulding at the base. The feet are capped with shoes of bronze and strengthened with bent right-angle braces. At the bottom of the walls, on the underside, are strips of ivory which follow the bends of the braces and fit into slots on the inner sides of the bronze shoes. Two gilded mushroom-shaped knobs, one on the lid and the other on an end panel, served as terminals for a tie which could not be undone without breaking the seal covering the knot. Each knob bears within a shrine-shaped frame the cartouche of Tutankhamun mounted on the hieroglyphic sign for 'gold' (*nub*) and flanked by uraei wearing either the double crown

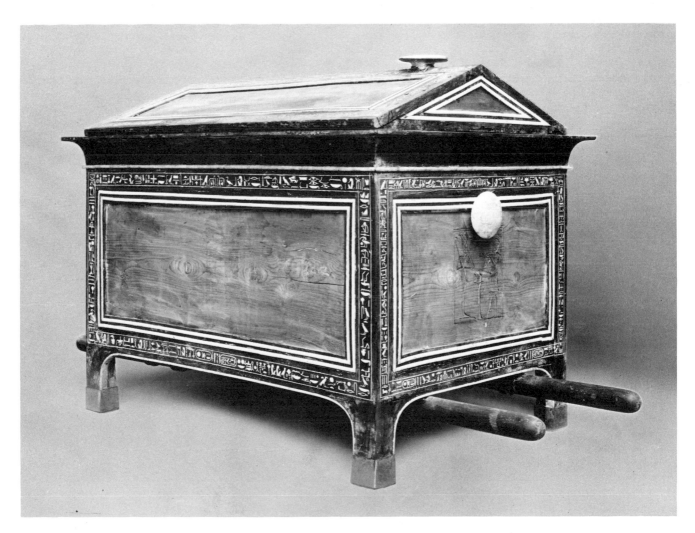

(left uraeus) or the crown of Lower Egypt (right uraeus). Both the uraei have pendent 'life' signs (*ānkh*) at the base of their hoods.

Unlike the other chests found in the tomb this chest, no doubt because of its size and weight when full, was provided with four poles so that it could be carried by bearers on their shoulders. Each pole slides backwards and forwards through two bronze rings, attached to boards which are fixed to the bottom of the box. A collar at the back end of the pole, greater in circumference than the ring, prevents the pole from slipping forward through the inner ring. When the chest

was not being carried, the poles could be pushed back until the collars of two axially opposite poles were touching each other and the poles were then entirely concealed from view. Portable chests of this kind are represented in relief on the walls of the *mastaba* tombs of high officials, such as Mereruka and Ankhmahor at Saqqara, dating from about a thousand years before the time of Tutankhamun. No other example of an actual portable chest is known.

Carved in low relief on one end of the chest within a rectangular frame, the top of which is in the form of the hieroglyphic sign for 'heaven', are figures of the king

and a god facing each other and separated by a vase on a stand. The king, whose ear is pierced for an earring (see no 39), wears the blue crown (see no 22) with uraeus and streamers, a broad collar and bracelets, and a kilt with apron. In his outstretched hands he offers the god a lamp and a pot of unguent. The lidded vase on the stand is of the same shape as some blue faience vessels found in the tomb, apart from the spout which, in this representation, is in the form of an ostrich feather signifying 'truth, justice' (*maāt*). According to a hieratic inscription on the box which contained those vessels, they were called by the name *nemset*, which must apply also to this vase,

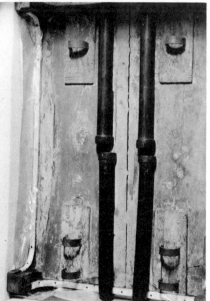

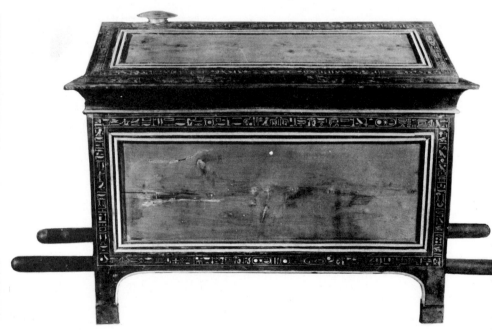

although its shape does not correspond exactly with that of *nemset* vases dating from earlier times. When figured in ritual scenes carved on temple walls, they contain cold water for libations. The god, called in the accompanying inscription 'Onnophris, who is at the head of the West, the great god, lord of the Necropolis' is only another form of Osiris. On his head he wears the *atef* crown with ostrich plumes and the uraeus. The artificial beard strapped to his chin is exceptionally long and straight. His body, as regularly, is shrouded in a long white garment from which his hands protrude, one holding a long crook and the other a flail, the regular insignia of Osiris. Under his feet is a pedestal in the form of a hieroglyphic sign which has the same sound-value and meaning as the ostrich feather. It is noticeable that the king is described in the hieroglyphic inscription as 'the Osiris, Nebkheperure', which shows that the action which he was performing was conceived as taking place after his death (see no 13).

The funerary character of the chest is further demonstrated by the inscriptions. Bands of text, incised and filled with yellow paint, on both the lid and the box consist, in the main, partly of utterances by various deities and partly of offering formulae. The gods who deliver the utterances – Thoth, Geb, Harendotis, Horakhty and Ptah-Seker-Osiris – promise the king *inter alia* that his mouth, his eyes and his ears will be opened, that his limbs will be rejuvenated, that heaven will receive his soul and earth his body, and

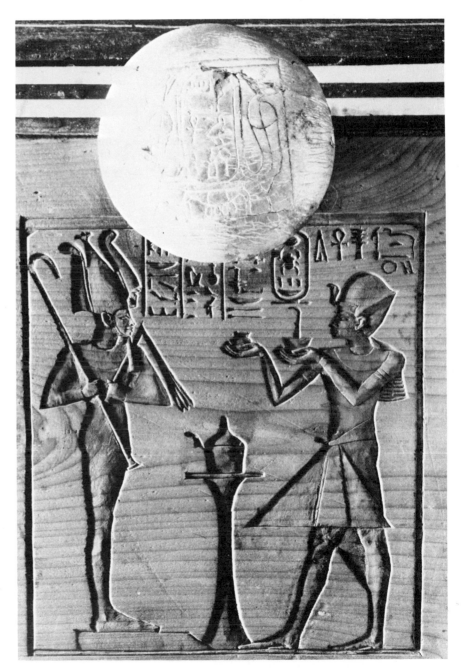

that he will be granted all kinds of sustenance. In the offering formulae the gods – Geb, Horakhty-Atum, Osiris-Onnophris and the divine Enneads – assure the king that, in return for the offerings presented to them, he will enjoy the sweet cool breeze, wine and the odour of incense, he will assume, like the sun-god, any form he chooses, he will be in the company of the gods in the bark of his father, Re, he will be reborn daily like the sun, he will live as long as the sun and will

be granted all the other benefits which can be accorded to a king when he is among the blessed dead.

Four columns of inscription at the gable ends of the lid name not only the king but also 'the Great Royal Wife, his beloved, the Mistress of the Two Lands, Ankhesenamun'.

This chest was found on the floor of the Antechamber in front of the lion-bed (see no 13). It had been stripped of its original contents by the tomb-robbers and refilled

with vessels and a miscellaneous collection of other objects, including stone knives, the lid of a rush basket, lumps of resin, balls of incense and dried fruits.

Length 83.0 cm, width 60.5 cm, height 63.5 cm.

Carter 1: 114, pls XVI, XVII, LV; Desroches-Noblecourt 58; Baker 94, fig 115; Paris Exh no 26.

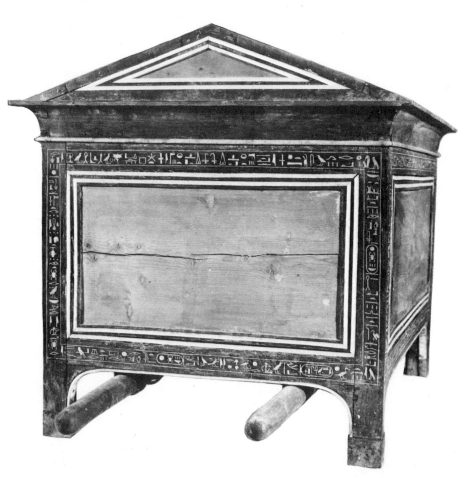

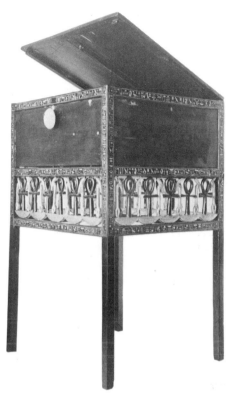

In design this cabinet resembles many pieces of European furniture dating from recent times, and yet its general style already had a long history even in the time of Tutankhamun. Wall-paintings in the tomb of an official named Hesire at Saqqara (*c* 2650 BC) show cabinets which differ in detail only from Tutankhamun's cabinet. No doubt the design owes its longevity to the simple fact that it satisfies both aesthetic and practical requirements.

The entire framework, including the long slender legs, is made of ebony and the inset panels are made of a reddish-brown wood which is probably cedar. The lid folds back on bronze hinges fixed to the top rail of the back of the cabinet. Gilded mushroom-shaped knobs, one on the front of the lid and the other on the front panel of the box, served as terminals for the knotted and sealed fastening cord. Both knobs bear the king's cartouches mounted on the hieroglyphic sign for 'gold' and flanked by crowned uraei with pendent 'life' signs, but the inscriptions are not identical, the lid-knob having his throne name, Nebkheperure, and the box-knob his birth-name, Tutankhamun. Internally the box is divided into compartments. Stretchers or crossbars placed at the mid-point help to give rigidity to the legs. The space between these stretchers and the bottom rails of the box is occupied with openwork bands consisting of black ebony 'life' signs and gilded 'prosperity' signs standing on gilded 'basket' signs signifying 'all'.

Hieroglyphic inscriptions filled with yellow pigment are incised on the entire framework of the lid and upper half of the cabinet as far as the tops of the legs. Those on the lid read from the front to the back and in this respect show the same orientation as the inscription on the lid of the bow-fronted chest no 17. All alike are bombastic formulae and self-glorifications of a kind greatly favoured by Egyptian kings. Some emphasize his divine nature, *eg* 'Son of Amun, begotten of the Bull of his Mother, he whom Mut, mistress of heaven, nursed and whom she suckled with her [own] milk, he whom the Lord of the Thrones of the Two Lands created to be ruler of that which the sun encircles, he [*ie* Amun] has assigned to him the throne of Geb and the powerful office of Atum'. Others extol his achievements as king, *eg* 'Maker of monuments, so that they came into existence at once, to his fathers and all the gods. He built their temples anew, he made their statues of fine gold, he provided their offerings on earth'. This claim was certainly not without substance, but the same cannot be said of another assertion in which he describes himself as 'a mighty king who subdued foreign lands, capturing those to the south and trampling down those to the north and slaughtering [his] enemies'. To the same category belong the words: 'He is Re-Atum and [?] the one who drove out evil from the temple of Re in (?) Heliopolis, purifying it [?] as it was at the beginning of time'.

Although it is true that these inscriptions are largely hyperbolical, they nevertheless show how completely Tutankhamun had restored the pre-Amarna pantheon. Not only is his relationship to the older gods affirmed, but in the central inscription on the lid he asserts that he is 'beloved of Amon-Re, king of the gods'. Aten too is mentioned, but only as one among many, although in one place the king calls himself 'the eldest son of Aten in heaven'.

This cabinet was found in the Annexe, robbed of its original contents; they had been replaced by four headrests, one being the ivory specimen shown in the exhibition (no 37).

Length 43.5 cm, width 40.0 cm, height 70.0 cm.

Carter III: 115–16, pl XXXVA; Desroches-Noblecourt 93, pl L; Baker frontispiece, 91–2, fig 106; Quibell pls XVII, XVIII; Yoyotte 123.

▷ Colour

Both in form and in construction this wooden chair is typical of its period. The curved back, set at a backward slant, is supported behind by three vertical stiles, one in the middle and one at each side, all joined to the top-rail and the back of the frame of the seat. The five wooden slats of the seat are curved with a double cove and fastened to the sides of the frame by means of mortise and tenon joints reinforced by bronze or copper rivets capped with gold. Similar joints are used throughout. Curved wooden brackets overlaid with strips of ivory strengthen the base joints of the front uprights of the armrests and the two stiles on the flanks. The legs, shaped like a lion's paws with inlaid claws of

ivory, stand on beaded drums shod with metal. Rounded stretchers, ornamented with papyrus flower terminals of ivory and fixed to the middle of the legs, help to keep the chair rigid and serve as a base for the latticework bracing between them and the frame of the seat.

The top-rail and the back-support are decorated with ivory marquetry of geometric designs broken by a frieze of single floral petals and lotus buds, which covers the upper crosspiece of the frame surrounding the back panel. The panel itself is overlaid on both its concave and its convex faces with broad upright strips of ivory and ebony arranged alternately and separated by narrow borders of the

same material. In contrast with this formal decoration the armrests have gilded inner panels adorned with scenes of a naturalistic kind. Although not absolutely identical in detail, the outer faces of the two panels show a recumbent ibex with one front and one back paw raised and the head turned back over its shoulder, and a desert plant within a border of continuous spirals. The inner faces are entirely devoted to desert plants enclosed in a striated border.

Although the chair bears no inscription, its inclusion in Tutankhamun's tomb furniture leaves little room for doubt that it was made for him when he was a child. A chair almost identical in its overall

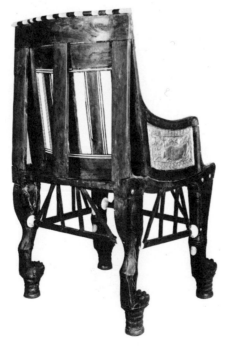

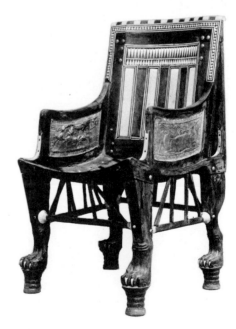

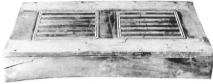

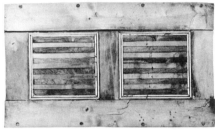

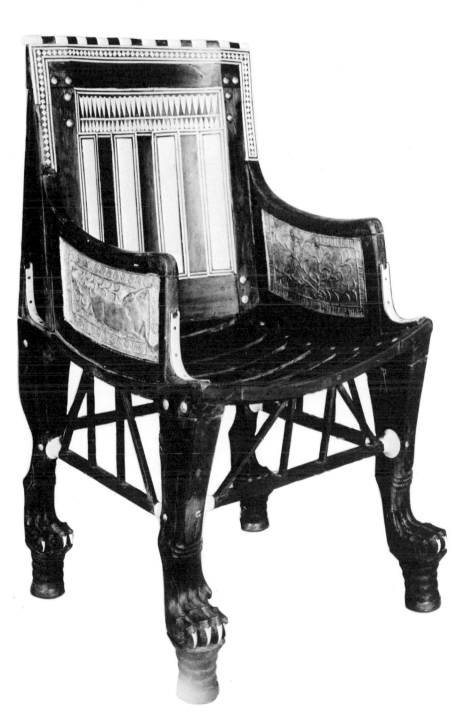

dimensions was made for Sitamun, a
daughter of Amenophis III and Queen Tiy,
but its decoration was more elaborate and
it was gilded, the whole appearance being
more typical of a piece of royal furniture
than Tutankhamun's chair. If they were
brother and sister, as some authorities
believe, the difference in richness would be
unexpected.

The small wooden footstool inlaid with
ivory shown with this chair was found
separately, but also in the Antechamber,
and there is nothing to prove that they
were associated. Both pieces of furniture
are said to be made of ebony, a material
which the Egyptians imported from
Africa. Patches of sound timber have been
inserted in the longer sides of the footstool
to replace blemished wood.

CHAIR
Height 71.12 cm, width 36.83 cm,
depth 39.37 cm.
FOOTSTOOL
Height 5.5 cm, width 23.5 cm,
length 36.5 cm.

Carter I: 114, pl LIX; Baker 84–6, fig 99;
Singer *et al* I: 686, fig 485B; Paris Exh
no 13.

As early as the First Dynasty (*c* 3000 BC) the Egyptians had mastered the technique of applying a veneer of fine wood to an inner layer of wood of inferior quality. Many examples of such veneers dating from the period between the beginning of historical times and the Eighteenth Dynasty have been found, and their number indicates that the method was frequently adopted by craftsmen in the manufacture of furniture and *objets d'art*. In this box the inner layer, which is only visible on the inside, consists of a stout frame and very thin boards, both of a light-coloured wood coated with a film of gesso and painted yellow; the whole of the exterior is overlaid with a veneer of ebony and a red wood which has not been identified. The boards of the floor and back are laid horizontally and those of the curved front vertically. The veneer is attached to the inner layer by a black resinous substance and pegged with small wooden dowels, except in the lid, where metal rivets capped with ivory are used. Four bronze handles (one missing) were fixed, two on each side, near the top of the box. The detachable lid is held firmly in position by a batten on the underside with a convex outer edge, which fits into a concave channel at the top of the interior of the back of the box. A connecting string wound round the mushroom-shaped ebony knobs on the lid and box with the two ends tied and sealed would prevent the lid from being opened without cutting the string or breaking the seal.

A difficult problem, for which no satisfactory solution has yet been found, is the purpose of a box of this shape. Carter recorded what he found in it as 'a higgledy-piggledy mess of cloth thrown together anyhow, certainly nothing to do with the original contents ... There were three gauntlets, two or three loincloths, but for the most part the material was medical, including a fingerstall and a sling (?) in addition to various-sized bandages.' A hieratic docket written in ink on the outside of the lid describes its contents as 'The *khetkhet* of king Nebkheperure, given life, preservation and health, which are in the funeral procession'. The meaning of the vital word *khetkhet* (which is in the plural) is, however, unknown and consequently the putative information vouchsafed by the docket is rendered nugatory. The hieroglyphic inscriptions on the ebony bands give only the names of Tutankhamun and Ankhesenamun, their titles and some of the king's bombastic epithets; they do not refer to the box itself or to its contents. Both the hieroglyphic inscription on the lid and the hieratic docket are written to be read from the back of the box, but no special significance need be attached to this feature. A similar orientation of the inscriptions may be seen in the cabinet, no 15. The wide ebony panel in the centre of the front is divided into two halves: in the upper half, beneath the hieroglyphic sign for 'heaven' are three cartouches, the middle bearing the personal name of Tutankhamun and the epithet Ruler of Southern On, the right his throne-name Nebkheperure, both surmounted by the sun's disk and ostrich plumes, and the left the name of his queen

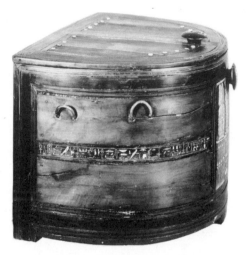

Ankhesenamun, surmounted by the sun's disk and two high feathers of a kind sometimes worn by queens in their headdresses; the lower half is filled with the symbol of the unification of the Two Lands (see nos 3 and 20). The suggestion has been made that the box was intended to hold rolls of papyri placed on end and inscribed with the prevailing code of laws. Such an explanation seems improbable. Nevertheless it is likely that it belonged to the furniture of the palace, for there is nothing either in its shape or in its hieroglyphic inscriptions to suggest that it was made for funerary purposes.

Close examination of the knob on the front of the box will show that the cartouche which now bears the name of Tutankhamun originally bore a different inscription. The surviving traces of the erased signs are sufficient to enable the

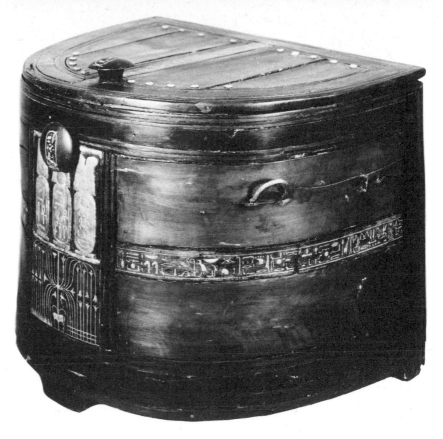

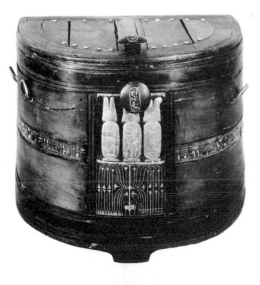

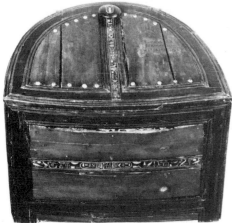

name Neferneferuaten and the epithet Wanre to be read with certainty. Neferneferuaten was the throne-name adopted by Tutankhamun's predecessor, whose personal name was Smenkhkare, when Akhenaten appointed him as co-regent some two or three years before his death. Several pieces of Tutankhamun's funerary equipment were originally made for the tomb of Smenkhkare (see no 9), but in this instance it seems very probable that the craftsman merely used a knob which had once been intended for a box belonging to his predecessor and was never required. The knob on the lid, which is inscribed with the throne-name of Tutankhamun, shows no trace of an erased inscription and the same applies to all the other cartouches on the box.

The box was found on the cow-bed (no 13) in the Antechamber and the lid in the Annexe, where it must have been cast by the ancient robbers.

Height 28.0 cm, width 37.1 cm, depth 32.7 cm.

Carter I: pls XVIII and XIX; Baker pl 87; Paris Exh no 23.

In the introduction to chapter 17 of the Book of the Dead, playing a game called *senet* is described as one of the occupations of the deceased person in the Next World and the vignette which accompanies the chapter represents him seated, often in the company of his wife, at a chequerboard but without an opponent. Like so many other activities ascribed to the Next Life, playing this game was also something which the deceased had done in his lifetime. It must have had a long history, because it is represented occasionally in the scenes on the walls of Old Kingdom tombs, a thousand years before the time of Tutankhamun, sometimes in association with music and other kinds of entertainment. On the standard board there were generally three rows of ten squares, five of which might be inscribed with hieroglyphics, and the playing pieces, frequently conical in shape, numbered five or seven for each player.

To judge from the number of boards in Tutankhamun's tomb, the game must have been one of his favourite pastimes. The boards – four in all – vary in size from a miniature set to the largest and most elegant, which is shown in this exhibition. It is box-shaped and is mounted in a rebate on top of an ebony stand in the form of a bed-frame with feline paws which rest on gilded drums. Beneath the drums is an ebony sledge. The claws of each paw are made of ivory and the 'cushions' and the braces, which strengthen the joints between the frame and the paws, are gilded. The box itself is veneered with ebony and the thirty squares, five of which

are inscribed, are inlaid with ivory. At one end of the board is a small drawer for the gaming-pieces. Originally it was fastened by two bolts, probably of gold, which slid into staples fixed on the frame. Since the pieces were missing, Carter supposed that they were made of gold and silver and were stolen by the ancient robbers.

Like many of the other known examples, this box is double-sided, the game played on the reverse side being called *tjau*, a word which seems to mean 'thieves'. This board is divided into twenty squares, a middle row of twelve squares flanked by four squares on each side at one end. Three of the squares in the middle row are inscribed, one with a kneeling figure of Ḥeḥ, the god of millions of years, another with two thrones in pavilions (the sign for a jubilee festival) and the third with the hieroglyphic signs for life, stability and welfare. Nothing is known with certainty about the rules of play for either game, but it is believed that the aim of each player in *senet* was to be the first to reach the square at the angle of the L-shaped arrangement inscribed with three signs meaning 'happiness, beauty'. The square preceding it may have been a hazard, because its hieroglyphs represent water. Certainly it was a game of chance, the moves being determined by the throw either of knuckle-bones or of four casting-sticks, both of which were found in the tomb. The casting-sticks were of two kinds, one pair having ends in the form of the tips of human fingers and the ends of the other being carved in the form of a long-eared canine animal, probably a fox. Both pairs

▷ Colour

consist of black ebony in the upper half and white ivory in the lower half. Perhaps the number of points scored from a cast depended on the number of sticks which finished with the white side or the black side uppermost when they were cast.

Besides the reference in the Book of the Dead to the game of *senet*, another religious text mentions what appears to be the same, or at least a very similar, game played by the deceased against a divine opponent to decide his fate in the Underworld. The extant versions of this text all date from later than the time of Tutankhamun, but they may preserve an ancient belief. Nothing, however, in the character of his boards suggests that they were specially intended for religious or funerary purposes. The incised inscriptions filled with yellow pigment on the sides and ends of this box are strictly mundane, wishing the king life and prosperity and employing such titles and epithets as 'The Strong Bull, beautiful of birth, image of Re, precious offspring [literally 'egg'] of Atum, King of Upper and Lower Egypt, ruler of the nine bows [ie foreign lands], lord of all the lands and possessor of might Nebkheperure'. On the other side he is called 'Goodly of laws, he who pacifies the Two Lands, the Horus of Gold exalted of crowns who placates the gods'. The short inscriptions around the drawer, which are of the same kind, describe him as 'The Good God, Lord of the Two Lands, lord of crowns whom Re created' and 'Beloved of all the gods, may he be healthy, living for ever'.

The four component parts of this piece were found scattered about the Annexe.

BOARD
Length 46.0 cm, width 16.0 cm, height 8.1 cm.
SLEDGE
Length 55.0 cm, width 17.5 cm.
SLEDGE AND STAND
Height 20.2 cm.

Carter III: 130–2, pl LXXV; Baker 99, fig 126; Desroches-Noblecourt 95, pl XLIX; Needler 74; Pieper 16–33.

Two inscriptions in the lower part of this palette show that it was made for the 'Princess Merytaten, daughter of the Great Royal Wife Nefertiti' who married Tutankhamun's predecessor Smenkhkare. At the top are six oval cavities filled with partly used pigments: white, yellow, red, green, blue and black, the six basic colours employed by the ancient Egyptians. The empty oblong slot was intended for brushes made of rushes.

Merytaten was the eldest daughter of Akhenaten and Nefertiti and a sister of Tutankhamun's queen Ankhesenamun. Since she bears the title 'Princess' and her name is not written in a cartouche, her husband, Smenkhkare, was probably not Akhenaten's co-regent at the time when this palette was made. If she was still alive at the time of Tutankhamun's death she was a widow, and it is surprising that she should have chosen as a gift to his tomb equipment an object made in the days of her childhood. Perhaps she had given it to Tutankhamun in her lifetime and it was placed in his tomb with his other personal possessions.

Egyptian scribes wrote in ink of two colours, usually in black but in red to

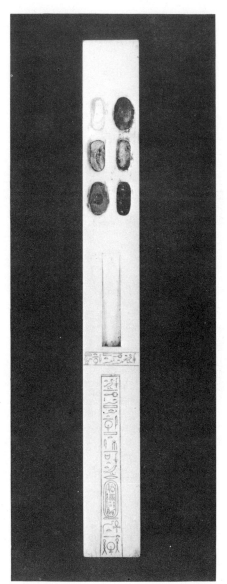

indicate headings of chapters in religious books, totals of numbers in accounts and anything considered hostile or unlucky. These palettes were provided with two cavities for cakes of dry paint (ink and paint were the same substance), the upper cavity for black and the lower for red. The tomb contained a number of palettes of this kind, and in addition some imitation palettes intended for ritualistic purposes. As a symbol the palette was closely associated with Thoth, the god of writing and wisdom. A spell in the Book of the Dead (94) puts in the mouth of the deceased person the words 'bring me the ink-pot and the palette, Thoth's writing equipment, and the secrets which belong to them'.

Merytaten's palette, which may also have possessed a magical significance, is clearly not a scribe's palette but a painter's, as the six colours in the cavities show, such as an artist would have used when painting the illustrations of a papyrus. It was found in the Treasury, laid between the paws of a jackal mounted on a shrine. There is nothing to indicate that this position had any special purport.

Not all the pigments have been analysed, but their probable identifications are white: sulphate of lime; yellow: orpiment; red: ochre; green: malachite; blue: frit; black: carbon.

Length 21.9 cm, width 2.5 cm, depth 0.7 cm.

Carter III: 45, p. XXIIA; Fox 27, pl 40E; Paris Exh no 9.

Egyptian stools fall into two main classes, folding and rigid. Within each class there is a wide variety of patterns, ranging from the simple to the elaborate, many of which are represented in the furniture found in the tomb of Tutankhamun. Although no actual example of the folding stool is included in this exhibition, two illustrations of the king seated on such a stool with a cushion may be seen on the sides of the gold shrine (no 25). In a third scene on the left-hand door of the same shrine he is shown seated on a rigid stool which is also provided with a cushion. A fine distinction cannot be drawn between the different uses of stools and chairs in ancient Egypt, but in the time of Tutankhamun chairs are more common in representations of formal occasions and stools in scenes of the ordinary activities of daily life.

The wood of which this stool is made has not been identified with certainty, but it is believed to be acacia, one of the very few kinds of timber grown in Egypt which were suitable for furniture. It is painted white apart from the grille, stretchers, feet and cartilagenous protuberances on the legs, all of which are gilded. Under the feet, the ringed drums are capped with metal, either copper or bronze. The double cove seat is bordered on the outer edges by a narrow cornice which contributes to the lightness and elegance of the piece. It is the gilded grille, however, which is the most distinctive feature of the stool. On all four sides it consists of the hieroglyphic sign for 'unification' *(sma)*, to which are tied the stems of the lotus and papyrus flowers.

It is a motif which is regularly found on the sides of the seats in royal monuments, sometimes with figures of two deities, representing Upper and Lower Egypt, holding the ends of the stems. As a symbol it commemorated the unification of the Two Lands (*ie* Upper and Lower Egypt) under Menes, the first king of the First Dynasty (see no 3). In ancient times the papyrus plant flourished in the marshes of the Delta and the artist has suggested this natural setting by showing the stems of the flowers emerging from a row of leaves at the base. The corresponding feature at the base of the lotus stems represents a plot of land divided by irrigation channels, the canals being the natural habitat of the lotus in Upper Egypt. As a hieroglyphic sign it is sometimes used to indicate the general sense of the Egyptian word for Upper Egypt *(shemā)*. The stretchers under the grille are decorated with the striated design found on the borders of the inner gilded panels of the chair no 16.

In one respect this stool, apart from being a seat, resembles a chair: the front

and the back are easily distinguishable, the front being the face which corresponds with the direction in which the feline feet are pointed. In decoration there is no difference between the two faces except that the lotus and papyrus flowers are on opposite sides of the *sma* sign and therefore back to back. This arrangement shows that the stool was intended to be placed facing eastwards so that the papyrus would be on the northern side and the lotus on the southern side.

Although it is solidly built, with mortise and tenon joints strengthened by metal pegs capped with gold, it has suffered some distortion from the strain of being tightly wedged between a bedstead and the wall of the Annexe where it had been thrown by the ancient robbers in their hurried operations in the tomb.

Height 45.0 cm, width 45.0 cm, depth 43.0 cm.

Carter III: 114, pl LXVIIIB; Desroches-Noblecourt 93, pl IVA; Baker 87, pl VIII; Paris Exh no 14.

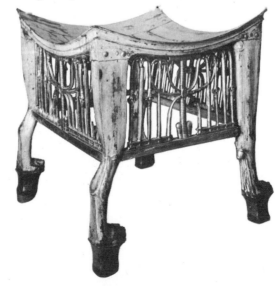

▷ Colour

Both artistically and technically this wooden chest is undoubtedly one of the outstanding pieces not only in this exhibition but in the whole collection of objects found in the tomb of Tutankhamun. No more than four pieces, of which two are this chest and the small golden shrine (no 25), show the king and queen together in a style reminiscent of so much of the art of the preceding Amarna Period but different in theme. Perhaps the most striking difference is that Akhenaten and Nefertiti are generally represented participating almost as equal partners in the performance of some activity, whereas the role of Ankhesenamun tends to be rather subservient, that of an intimate companion who attends to Tutankhamun's needs. The relationship between king and queen is nearer to that of a nobleman and his wife as it is portrayed in some of the painted tombs of the pre-Amarna Period at Thebes, but it is not identical because the nobleman's wife is represented merely as an onlooker.

In its design the chest embodies the main architectural elements of the standard Egyptian cabin-shaped shrine, except insofar as the main dimension is horizontal and not vertical. The lid

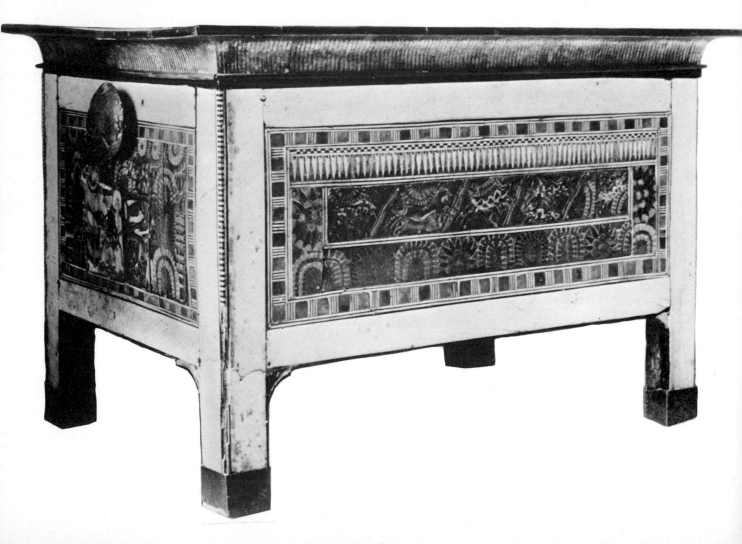

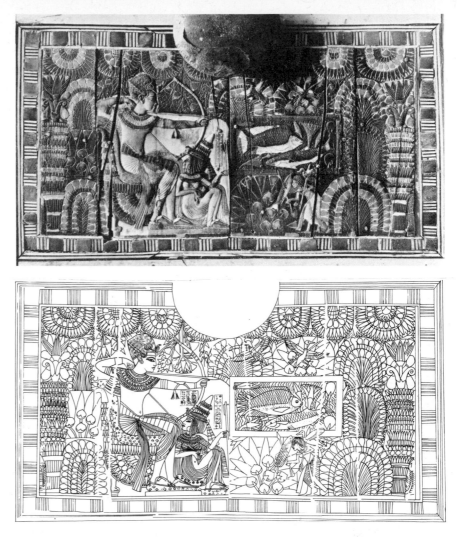

(judged to be too fragile for inclusion in this exhibition) is an elongated adaptation of the hunchbacked roof. The entablature consists of a cavetto cornice overlaid with gilded gesso and edged with ebony, a wooden torus-moulding painted dark green and a narrow ebony frieze. On the ledge above the cornice is an inlaid band consisting of red and blue plaques, the former of painted calcite and the latter of glazed composition, arranged alternately and separated by black and white striped plaques apparently made of ebony and ivory. A similar band of decoration serves as a border to the painted scenes carved in ivory panels on the outer faces of the four walls, each scene being set within a frame composed of broad strips of plain ivory which veneer the corner uprights and transverse members above and below the panels. The feet are capped with ferrules of bronze or copper.

In virtue of its position, and also of its character, the principal scene is undoubtedly the one carved in low relief on the panel at the head end of the chest which depicts Tutankhamun shooting with bow and arrow wild fowl and fish from the bank of a rectangular pond. In accordance with a common artistic convention, part of the string of the bow and the butt-end of the arrow are concealed behind the king's head and body while his right hand, which holds them, is shown in the position which it would occupy if the string were on the near side of his head (cf, however, nos 23 and 25). His extended left arm is protected by an archer's leather bracer from injury through friction caused by the string. He is seated on a curved-back chair with a cushion and his feet rest on a cushioned footstool. He wears the blue crown with uraeus and pendent streamers (see no 22), a broad bead collar and a pleated skirt tied

around the waist by a long sash, the ends of which reach nearly to the ground, and an apron which is also suspended from the waist. On his arms and wrists are broad bracelets and on his feet sandals. The lobe of his ear is pierced for an earring (see no 39). The queen squats on a cushion in front of the king holding a lotus flower in her right hand and an arrow, ready to pass to the king, in her left hand. Her dress also is pleated and tied around the waist by a sash with long ends. At the top of her wig is a fillet with uraeus and pendent streamers, surmounted by a diadem of uraei with sun's disks. Resting on the wig is a conical unguent-holder adorned with a floral circlet. The name and titles of the king (who bore the epithet 'beloved of Ptah, Lord of Truth') and those of the queen are engraved in the hieroglyphic inscriptions

in front of their figures. Beneath the pond is an attendant bearing a fish and a duck, each transpierced by one of the king's arrows.

As a background to this scene the artist has filled the entire field with festoons, garlands and bouquets in which the flowers and individual petals of the blue lily, buds of the white lotus and the leaves and fruit of the mandrake are predominant. Among other plants which are recognizable by their flowers and leaves are convolvulus, cornflowers and possibly a vine. Even the gap between the legs of the king's chair and the narrow aperture between the stiles and the back-rest are draped with flowers. Two upright bouquets, each surmounted by a lily palmette and a blue lily with supporting buds of the white lily, stand one at each side of the panel, giving the appearance of architectural columns and suggesting to the eye that the action is taking place under a bower. The whole composition is intended to convey the impression of the idyllic surroundings in which the king would lead his afterlife.

Very similar floral motifs are repeated on the sides and back of the chest, but their setting is entirely different. Each panel has, within its ribbon border, a frieze consisting of a black and white chequer-pattern band and white pendent petals on a blue and red background above a rectangular black and white frame, which is divided by three oblique wavy lines, coloured black, red and black, into five compartments on each side and two compartments at the end. Within these compartments are representations of animals, some being attacked by other animals and others without visible attackers. It is noticeable that the legs of the animals often cut across the dividing lines, but the floral backgrounds are kept inside the divisions. Beginning from the end with the panel already described, the following episodes are shown:

*Left side*
a spotted calf attacked by a white hound wearing a collar,
an ibex in flight,
a spotted calf in flight,
a spotted bull attacked by a cheetah which has jumped on its back,
an ibex attacked by a white hound wearing a collar.

*Back*
(right) an ibex attacked by a cheetah which has leapt on its back,
(left) a spotted bull attacked by a hound wearing a collar.

*Right side*
a spotted calf rising on its feet,
an ibex attacked by a lion,
a spotted bull in flight,
two spotted calves, one recumbent, the other running,
a spotted calf in flight with its hind legs in the air.

In character these scenes have much in common with those on the reverse side of the sheath of the gold dagger (no 36) and it is not inconceivable that they were drawn by the same draughtsman or at least by draughtsmen from the same workshop. At first sight they appear to have little connection with the scene on the front panel of the box, but the hound is clearly the royal hunting animal and, although the king himself is not shown, the whole composition gives the impression of being the hunting counterpart to the fowling and fishing scene in which it was necessary to represent the king as the archer whose

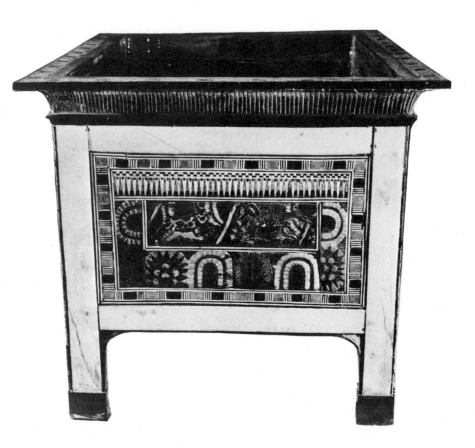

arrows secured the prey. In contrast with these lively scenes the representation on the lid of the young king, leaning slightly on a long staff and receiving bouquets of lotus and papyrus flowers from the queen, presents a blissful picture of peaceful domestic life.

Although this chest had been stripped of its contents by the ancient robbers and had been separated from its lid, so that the base was found in the north-west corner of the Annexe and the lid in the north-east corner, it may be deduced that it probably held some of the king's ceremonial robes. It was fastened, like other boxes in this exhibition, by a string tied round the gilded wooden knobs on the lid and the head-end of the base, the knot being sealed.

Length 72.0 cm, width 53.0 cm, height 48.5 cm.

Carter III: 118, frontispiece; Desroches-Noblecourt 95, pl 176; Baker 95-7, fig 117; Fox 32-3, pl 65; Yoyotte 125; Paris Exh no 24.

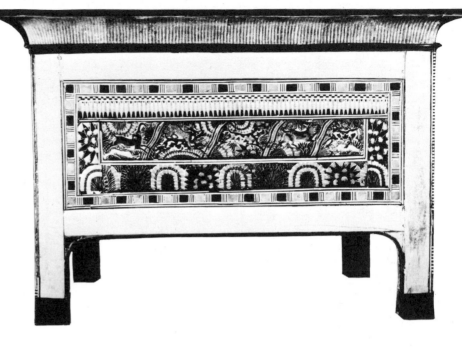

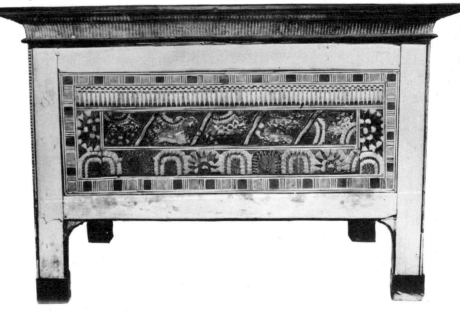

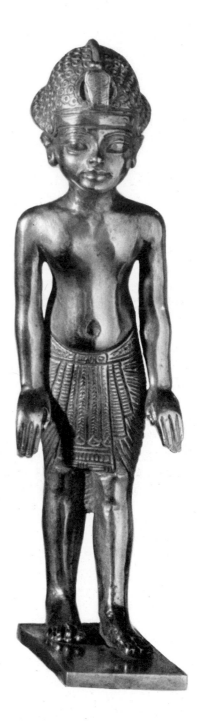

Among the many objects from this tomb which remain unparalleled in Egyptian art are two small figures of the king, one in gold and the other in silver, the feet in each case being socketed into a plate of the same metal as the figure. Beneath the plate is a tubular shaft of silver or of gold. They were found, wrapped in fine linen and bound together, on the floor between the two outermost shrines which protected the king's coffins. Apart from their material, the two figures are almost identical in every respect. The gold figure, which is shown here, is cast solid and chased. It shows the king wearing only the blue crown and a pleated kilt with ornamented apron suspended from a girdle. His throne-name is engraved on the clasp of the girdle. The upper part of the body and the feet are bare.

Nothing in the dress of the king indicates the purpose of the object. His crown *(khepresh)*, sometimes incorrectly called the war-helmet, first appears on monuments as a royal headdress at the end of the Seventeenth Dynasty and is commonly worn by Tutankhamun's predecessors in the Eighteenth Dynasty in many different circumstances: in battle, in religious and secular ceremonies and in private life. He is represented wearing the same kind of pleated kilt shooting ostriches from his chariot (no 23), in some of the scenes on the small gilded shrine (no 25) and on the gilded wooden figures (nos 26 and 27). The position of the hands, with their backs facing towards the front, is an exceptional feature in figures with a close-fitting kilt; normally this pose is found only when the kilt is of a different type with a triangular frontal projection. Perhaps this variation is but an extension of the regular practice of Egyptian sculptors, when carving in relief, of avoiding whenever possible depicting the hands in profile.

In form, this piece immediately suggests the standards carried by priests and officials in state and religious ceremonies. As a rule, however, such standards consist of a long stave surmounted by a cult-object resting on a flat base. The cult-objects include birds and animals sacred to particular gods and, exceptionally, even mummiform figures, but not human figures. Furthermore, the staves are considerably longer than those of this piece and its companion in silver. Possibly they were more in the nature of wands than standards, or conceivably marking-pegs used in some ceremony. The unmistakably childlike appearance of the king might suggest that the ceremony was his coronation, but why they should have been made of two different metals and how they were employed cannot be explained. Nevertheless his age and consequently his shortness of stature may account for the reduction in length of the stave.

Height 1.315 m.
Height of figure 9.0 cm.

Carter II: 35, pl VII; Desroches-Noblecourt 71, 176; Aldred 87, pl 155; Fox pl 23;

Paris Exh no 15; USA Exh no 15;
Japan Exh no 12.

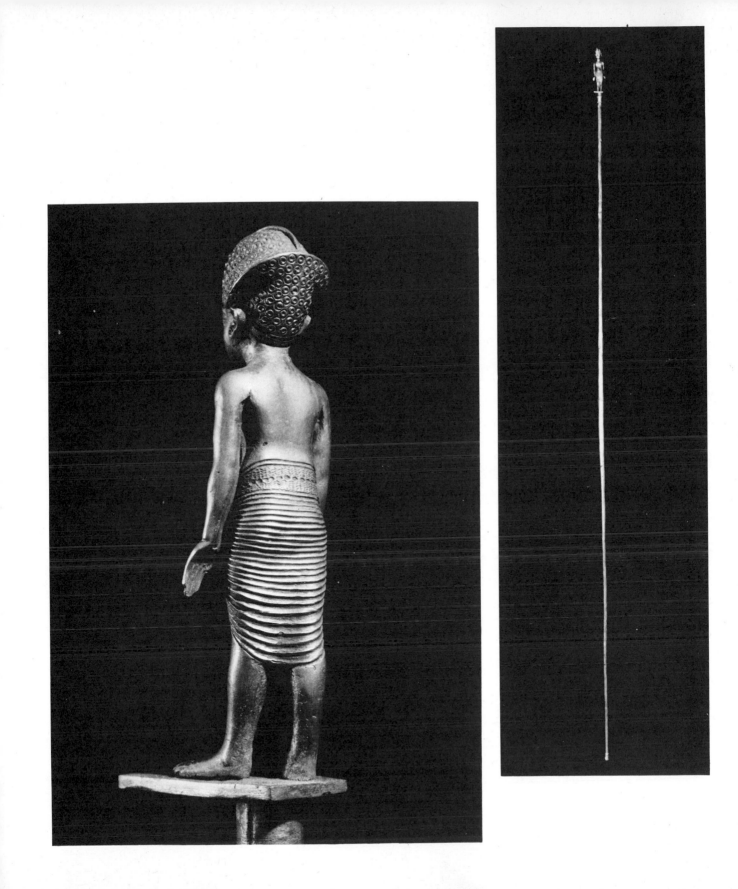

An inscription on the handle of this fan states that it is made of 'ostrich feathers obtained by His Majesty when hunting in the desert east of Heliopolis'. Stumps of the feathers may still be seen in the holes on the outer edge of the palm. When complete it consisted of fifteen white and fifteen brown feathers, arranged in alternate colours. The feathers had been almost entirely devoured by insects when it was found on the floor of the Burial Chamber between the two innermost of the four golden shrines which shielded the coffins of the king. It is made of wood covered with sheet-gold.

Embossed on each face of the palm are lively scenes of the king hunting the ostriches. On the obverse he is shown riding in his chariot and shooting with his bow at two ostriches, one of which is already on the ground. His Saluki hound, in hot pursuit, is about to dispatch the birds. The king wears a short wig with two streamers, a short leopard-skin corselet and a kilt with ornate apron. On his left wrist is an archer's leather bracer. In order that his hands may be free to use his bow, he has put the reins around his body. The richly caparisoned horses, depicted in full gallop, have closely trimmed manes, and ostrich plumes and sun's disks fixed to the headstalls of the bridles. An object, shaped like an animal's tail and suspended near the shoulder behind the girth, is found on horses of his period when decked for ceremonial occasions; its function is not clear and it may be merely decorative. The chariot is a light vehicle reminiscent of a curricle, made of wood and fitted with a sun's disk on the front of the pole. Two cases, one for bows, are strapped to the body of the chariot inside the wheels. The quiver for the arrows is suspended from the back of the king's girdle, its

handle resembling a long tail. Behind the chariot is the hieroglyphic sign for 'life' *(ānkh)*, with human hands and feet, carrying a fan of the same kind as this fan. The inscription above this composite figure 'may all protection of life attend him' *(ie* the king), although a common formula, is probably intended to emphasize the symbolical nature of the figure. Within the bow are two hieroglyphic signs meaning 'possessor of a strong arm', a regular epithet referring to a king, but here with special application to his strength with the bow. The remainder of the field is occupied with desert flowers, perhaps thistles, and the inscription: 'The Good God Nebkheperure, given life for ever like Re'.

On the reverse side of the palm the king is shown returning from the hunt. The spirited horses are held in check, the reins being now in the king's hands together with his bow and a whip. He himself has put on a long pleated garment and what appears to be a shoulder-wrap with 'feathered' fringes. The form of the 'feathers' does not suggest that they are ostrich plumes, as some writers have supposed. Two attendants in front of the chariot carry on their shoulders the two ostriches shot by the king. In view of the weight of these birds (about 345 pounds fully grown if they belong to the species *Struthio Camelus* L which existed in Egypt until some 150 years ago), it is not likely that the scene, at least in detail, is to be interpreted literally. The explanatory inscription, which fills most of the upper part of the field, reads: 'The Good God who secures [the quarry] in hunting, who strives (?) and engages in combat in every desert [or, 'who campaigns and fights against every foreign land'], who shoots to kill like [the goddess] Bastet, his horses are

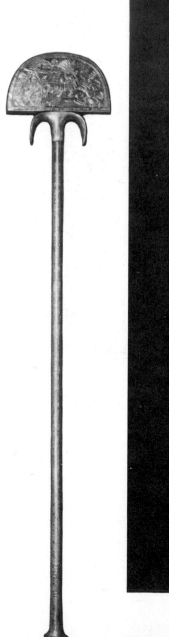

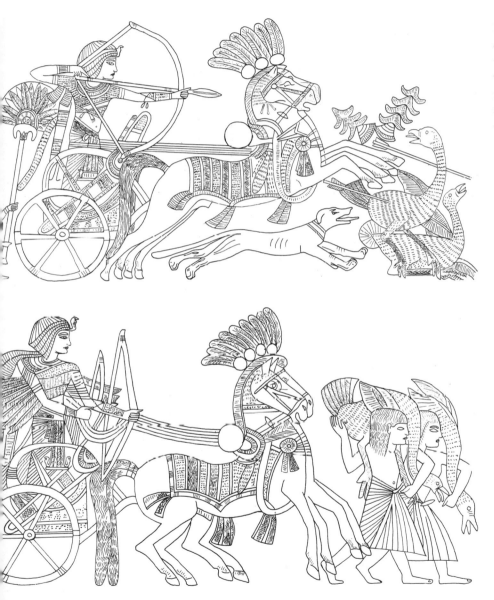

like bulls when they convey the King of Upper and Lower Egypt, the Lord of the Two Lands, possessor of a strong arm, Nebkheperure, given life for ever like Re'. The group of hieroglyphic signs immediately behind the quiver 'given all life' is probably to be taken separately and not as part of the main inscription.

Fans of this kind were regularly carried by attendants in royal processions at court and in religious ceremonies, their modern counterparts being the flabella borne in processions in Rome behind the Pope when seated on the *sedia gestatoria*. The characteristic features are the long handle terminating in a knob at the lower end and in a stylized papyrus or lotus flower at the top, a semicircular or elongated palm and several long ostrich plumes. They were used chiefly as sunshades. Another type of fan, carried as a symbol of office, generally had a shorter handle and a single ostrich plume.

Length of handle 95.0 cm. Height of palm 10.5 cm, width of palm 18.5 cm.

Carter II. 15, 16, 46, 242, 243, pls LXIA and LXII; Desroches-Noblecourt 71, 205, 298, pl XX; Fox pl 24; Paris Exh no 25.

▷ Colour

One of a pair of identical emblems found in the north-west and south-west corners of the Burial Chamber. The upper part, made of wood overlaid with gesso and gilded, represents a pole terminating in a lotus bud and an inflated animal-skin suspended on the pole by a copper wire tail ending in a papyrus flower. The base consists of a solid alabaster (calcite) stand in which the pole is fixed. Inscribed on the base are the name and titles of Tutankhamun 'given life for ever and ever' and the epithet 'Beloved of Anubis who presides over the embalming booth'.

In very remote times this fetish belonged to a god named Imiut, meaning 'He who is in his wrappings', who was eventually identified with Anubis the jackal-god of embalming. An early example, found in 1914 by the Metropolitan Museum of Art near the pyramid of Sesostris I (*c* 1971–1928 BC) at El-Lisht, was placed in a wooden shrine. Like the emblem in Tutankhamun's tomb, it consisted of a wooden rod and an alabaster stand, but the headless animal-skin was real and it was stuffed with linen. It was however wrapped in bandages like a mummy, linen pads being placed within the bandages as packing to fill the irregularities between the skin and the rod. The stand, which resembled a vessel, was about two-thirds full of a bluish-coloured substance, completely dried and considered to be some kind of ointment. It is easy to see how the god acquired the name 'He who is in his wrappings'. Tutankhamun's emblems represent a later development, not uncommon in Egyptian tomb

equipment, in which a model was used in place of the object itself.

Height 1.67 m.
Height of stand 20.0 cm; depth of stand maximum 23.5 cm, minimum 16.5 cm.

Carter II: 32, pls V, VI; Desroches-Noblecourt 250; Lythgoe 150–2.

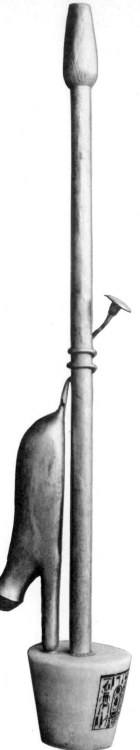

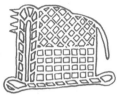

Some two thousand years before the time of Tutankhamun, the vulture goddess of Elkab, Nekhbet, was worshipped locally in an oblong pavilion made of a light wooden frame, the top of which was covered with the skin of an animal. The earliest representations, which date from about 3100 BC, show this pavilion in a stylized form, sometimes mounted on a sledge. Its roof frequently has a hump at the front and a downward slope towards the back (see above). It was called the Great House (*per wer*). When the rulers of Elkab succeeded in establishing their supremacy over the whole of Upper Egypt and ultimately, through Menes, in conquering Lower Egypt, Nekhbet was promoted to the position of joint tutelary goddess of the king of the Two Lands, her partner being the serpent goddess of Buto, Wadjet, who had advanced from local to national recognition under the former kings of Lower Egypt (see no 43). The sanctuaries of the two goddesses (called *iterty*) were then regarded as representative of the sanctuaries of all the local deities in their respective regions of the united kingdom. Thus, in the step pyramid enclosure of Zoser (c 2650 BC), two rows of dummy shrines faced each other in the jubilee festival court, one row for the gods of Upper Egypt in the form of the sanctuary of Nekhbet and the other row for the gods of Lower Egypt in the form of the sanctuary of Wadjet (*per nu*).

Tutankhamun's small shrine is in the form of the sanctuary of Nekhbet mounted on a sledge. It is made of wood overlaid with a layer of gesso and covered with

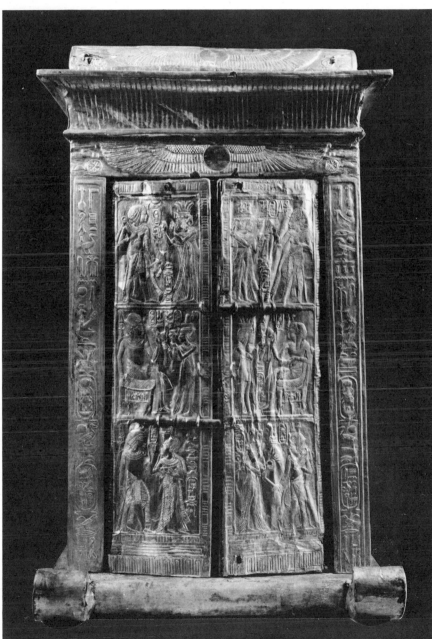

▷ Colour

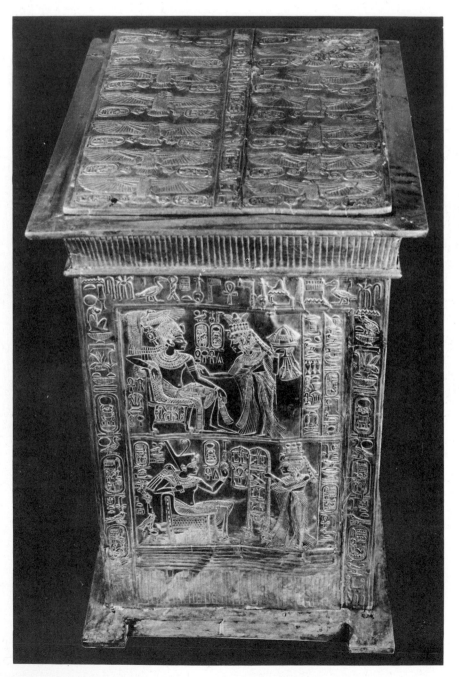

sheet gold. The wooden sledge is overlaid with silver. Carter was of the opinion that the gesso was first modelled in relief and the plain sheet gold was then pressed against it until it had registered the impression of the modelling, the outer face of the gold being finally chased. It seems doubtful, however, whether the gesso, even with skins of gossamer-like linen, which a recent examination has shown to be present on both faces of the exposed gesso on the inside of one of the doors, would have had the strength to withstand the amount of pressure and friction involved in the process. If this doubt is valid, the scenes and inscriptions must have been worked on the gold itself; the gold sheets would then have been put face downwards on a flat surface and covered with a piece of linen; lastly the gesso in a molten state would have been poured on the back of the linen so that it filled the depressions on the reverse side of the gold and, while it was still soft, the second piece of linen would have been applied to the outer surface. The purpose of the gesso would thus have been to give support to the decoration on the gold and to provide a flat surface for attachment to the wooden walls, roof and door.

Every exposed surface of the shrine is covered with scenes, inscriptions or some other kind of decoration, all in relief, of which the following are the principal:

ROOF
Fourteen figures of vultures of the goddess Nekhbet, with outstretched wings, are represented in relief on the top of the roof,

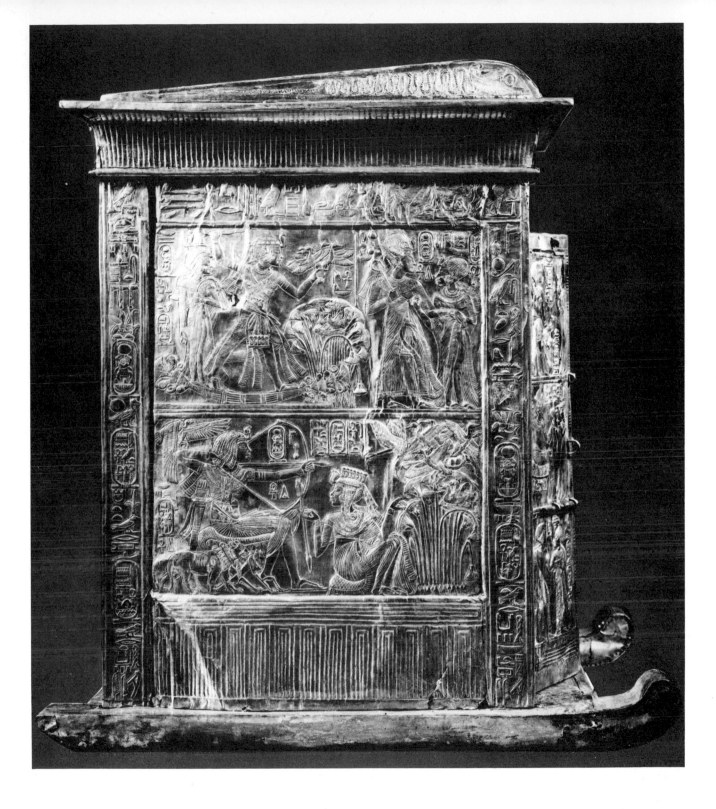

seven on each side of a single column of inscription giving the names and titles of the king and queen. The vultures hold in their talons the hieroglyphic sign for 'eternity' (*shen*). Cartouches bearing the names of either the king or the queen occupy the space at each side of the talons. On the front of the roof is the winged disk of Horus of Behdet, the place being named in the inscriptions at the tips of the wings. A winged uraeus with the 'eternity' sign between the wings occupies the entire length of each of the vertical sides of the roof.

FRONT

Beneath the roof on all four sides and projecting outwards at the top is a cavetto cornice with a torus moulding at the base. The whole of the front of the shrine is in the form of a doorway, the lintel of which is decorated with the winged disk of Horus of Behdet and the jambs bear inscriptions describing the king (left) as 'the son of Ptah and Sakhmet', and (right) as 'the image of Re who does what is beneficial to him who begat him'. In each case he is proclaimed as 'beloved of (the goddess) Urt Ḥekau', a name meaning 'The Great Enchantress', who is called in another inscription on the shrine 'Lady of the Palace'.

Each of the two doors is provided at the top and bottom with pivots, which fit into sockets, one in the lintel and the other in the floor of the sledge, and with a silver bolt which slides through two gold staples into a third staple in the other door. Two additional staples, side by side in the

middle of each door, were intended for a sealed tie. On the outer faces of the door are representations of incidents in the daily life of the king and queen, arranged in three panels on each door. The uppermost panel on the left-hand door shows the queen in a plumed headdress standing with hands upraised before the king, who holds in his right hand the crook and sceptre and in his left a lapwing (see no 34). In the corresponding panel on the right-hand door, and on both the middle panels, the queen holds out bunches of flowers towards the king and in the middle panel on the right she also holds a sistrum. The queen's headdress in two of these scenes is surmounted by a cone of unguent, flanked in one instance by uraei with the sun's disk. In the middle panels the king is seated on a stool (left) and on a chair (right), both with thick cushions. He wears the blue crown (see no 22) on the left and the *nemes* headdress on the right. In the bottom panels, on the left side, the queen holds the king's arm with both hands and, on the right, the king's hand with her left hand, while extending a blue lotus and buds towards him in her right hand.

The gold overlay from the inner face of the left-hand door is lost, but it is evident from the damaged impression on the surviving gesso that its decoration was very similar to that of the right-hand door. Sandwiched between two panels, which are entirely filled with the king's cartouches and supporting uraei, is another scene of the queen holding a bunch of flowers and a sistrum towards the king. In this case her headdress is surmounted by

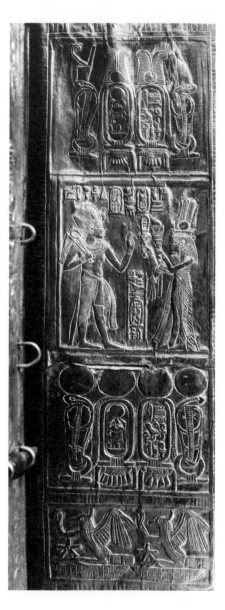

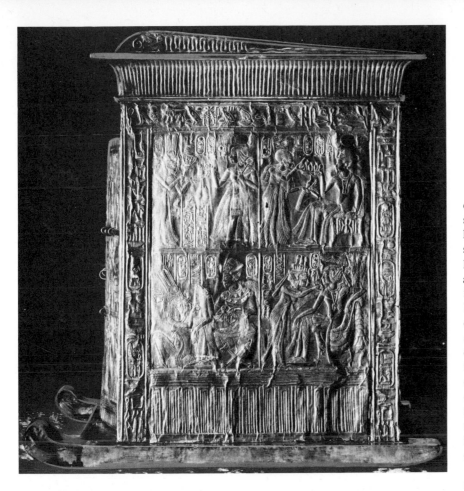

lyriform horns and the sun's disk with two high plumes. At the bottom are two lapwings with outstretched human arms, both mounted on the hieroglyphic sign for 'all' (*neb*) and having a five-pointed star (*dwa*) beneath the arms, thus forming a kind of monogram meaning 'adoration of all people' (see no 34).

SIDES

The top-rails and two stiles of both sides are inscribed with the names and titles of the king and queen, followed by the words 'beloved of the Great Enchantress' with or without the epithet 'Lady of the Palace'.

On the left side, in the upper register, the king stands in a boat made of papyrus stems throwing a boomerang, but the quarry – wildfowl rising from the papyrus marshes – is not shown (see no 21). The queen stands behind him as an onlooker; in her left hand she holds a flail or perhaps a fly-whisk. The king, who wears on the upper part of his body a corselet and over it two representations of falcons, holds in his left hand four birds which may represent his 'bag' or may be tame fowl used as decoys. In the clump of papyrus behind the prow of the boat can be seen a nest with two fledglings. The right-hand portion of this register is occupied with a scene which, although different in detail, repeats the theme of the bottom panel on the left-hand door. In the present setting it seems out of place.

A second fowling scene is represented in the lower register. The action is conducted not from a boat, but on the bank at the edge of a papyrus swamp. The king is seated on the stool with a thick cushion, his tame lion is by his side, and the queen squats on a cushion at his feet. Behind his head is the vulture of Nekhbet. He is in the act of shooting an arrow at birds rising from the swamp, one of which has already been hit. The string of his bow has been delineated by the artist as though it passed around the king's neck. His quiver hangs down behind him suspended on a strap from his shoulder. As in the similar scene on the head end of the chest no 21, the queen holds in her hand an arrow, ready to pass it to the king. With her other hand she seems to be pointing at the fledglings in the nest, perhaps urging the king to take care not to hurt them.

The other (right) side has four scenes, all of an unusual kind. In the left of the top register the queen extends towards the king a sistrum and a necklace with an elaborate counterpoise. At the front of the counterpoise are the head and shoulders of a goddess surmounted by cow's horns and the sun's disk and having the uraeus on her brow. Human hands project from beneath her collar, each hand holding towards the king a sign of 'life' (*ānkh*). The goddess may be Isis, Hathor or Mut, any one of whom may be called the Great Enchantress. In the inscription between the king and queen the following address is attributed to the queen: 'Adoration with offerings, may the Great Enchantress receive thee, O Ruler, beloved of Amun!'

In the second scene in the top register the king, seated on a cushioned chair, holds out a vessel containing flowers and

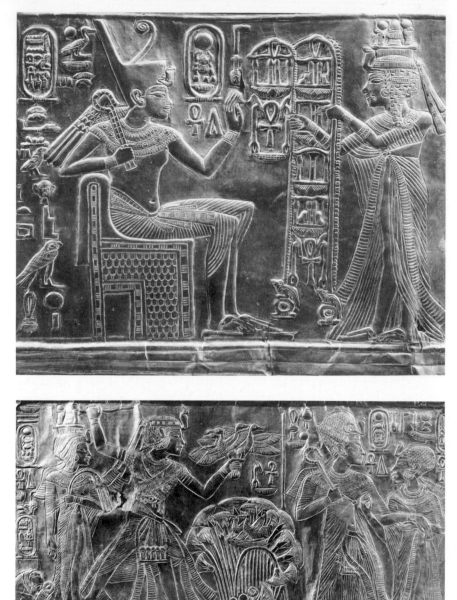

the queen pours water into the vessel from a vase in her right hand. In her left hand she holds a lotus flower and bud and a poppy.

On the left of the lower register the king pours water from a vessel into the cupped right hand of the queen. Her left elbow rests on his knee. The king, holding a bouquet of lotus flowers and poppies, sits on a stool covered with a cushion and an animal-skin. What appear to be balls under the claw feet are in reality the ends of rounded crossbars. In the right-hand scene the queen is tying the king's floral collar behind his neck while he sits in a chair which is festooned with flowers. Nekhbet's vulture hovers over his head.

BACK
Two scenes decorate the back. In the uppermost the queen stoops towards the king, her right hand touching his left arm. In her left hand she holds, in addition to a bunch of lotus flowers and buds hanging downwards, an unguent-cone holder mounted on a stand and decorated with lotus flowers. Apparently it is a replacement for the unguent-cone holder with plumes already on the queen's head above the crown of uraei.

In the lower scene the king, seated on a throne and wearing the crown of Lower Egypt, raises his left hand to receive from the queen two notched palm-ribs, the hieroglyphic signs for 'years'. Within these signs are the symbols for jubilee festivals and also amuletic signs in groups. They are attached at the bottom to single tadpoles – the sign for '100,000' – mounted on the sign for 'eternity'. The inscription behind the king reads: 'The Son of Re, Lord of Diadems, Tutankhamun has appeared in glory on the throne of Horus like Re'.

Of the contents of this shrine only a gilded wooden pedestal and back-support remained when it was found in the Antechamber. The pedestal still had the imprint of the foot of a statuette, very probably made of gold and certainly representing the king himself. A second statuette, representing the queen, may once have stood by its side.

SHRINE
Height 50.5 cm, width 26.5 cm, depth 32.0 cm.
SLEDGE
Length 48.0 cm, width 30.7 cm.

Carter I: 137, pl XXIX; Desroches-Noblecourt 66, pls VII–IX, LI; Fox pl 11; Baker 88–9, fig 104; Lange and Hirmer 464, pl XXXIII.

A row of black wooden shrines standing against the south wall of the Treasury housed thirty-two wooden figures of gods or of the king. There were twenty-two shrines, all except one with their doors closed and fastened with a cord and sealed. Three of the figures were coated with black resin (see no 1) and the remainder were gilded. Each figure was enveloped from the neck to the feet in a linen cloth marked in ink with the date of its manufacture and showing that they were all woven in the time of Akhenaten. Of the seven figures of the king found in the shrines three are displayed in this room (nos 26–28).

This figure is carved of a hard wood overlaid with gesso and gilded. The eyes are made of glass and the gilded uraeus is modelled in bronze. It represents the king wearing the crown of Lower Egypt, a bead collar, a pleated kilt with apron and a pair of sandals. The lobes of the ears are pierced for earrings (see no 39). In his right hand he holds a flail and in the left a long crooked staff, both these insignia, together with the sandals, being made of gilded bronze. In accordance with an artistic convention dating back to the beginning of Egyptian history, the left leg is placed in advance of the right. Compared with the rest of the figure, which is delicately carved, the legs are heavy, a common fault in Egyptian sculpture. The deep dip in the front of the girdle, which reveals much of the abdomen, is characteristic of Amarna art.

The wooden pedestal, which is varnished with black resin, is not inscribed.

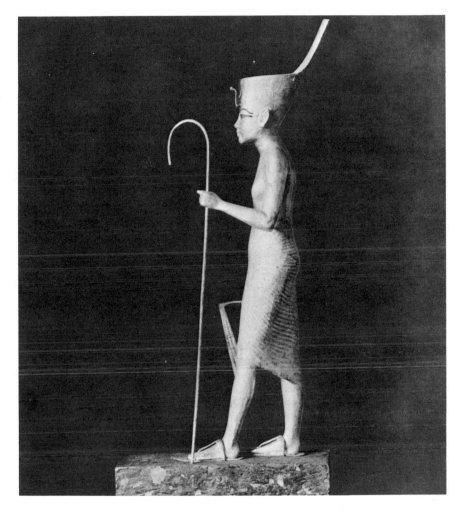

FIGURE
Height 62.0 cm.

PEDESTAL
Length 31.2 cm, width 12.0 cm, height 6.8 cm.

Carter III: 51–4, pl XIIA; Desroches-Noblecourt pls 159 and XLVI.

▷ Colour

Egyptian sculpture in the round, if it portrays a king or a queen, very seldom shows the subject performing an action, although representations in relief of kings engaged in religious and secular activities are very common (see nos 23 and 25). This piece, which shows the king harpooning from a boat made of papyrus stems, is an exception to the rule. It is one of a pair of similar figures found together in one of the black wooden shrines set against the south wall of the Treasury (see no 26). It was enveloped in a single sheet of linen extending from the shoulders to the ankles.

Carved in wood, the figure of the king is coated with gesso and gilded. Its eyes of glass (perhaps with pupils of obsidian) are set in bronze or copper sockets, the same metal being used for the eyebrows. The boat, also made of wood, is painted green apart from the bindings of the papyrus stems and the calices, both of which are gilded. Beneath the boat is a rectangular wooden pedestal varnished with black resin. The king wears the red crown of Lower Egypt, a bead collar, pleated kilt with apron and sandals. In his right hand he holds the harpoon and in his left a coil of rope. The uraeus, sandals, harpoon and rope are made of bronze, all except the rope being gilded.

In Pharaonic times hippopotami frequented the swamps and papyrus marshes of the Lower Nile; even as recently as the beginning of the last century the traveller W. J. Bankes recorded that a hippopotamus had reached the Delta, though at that time it must have been a very exceptional occurrence.

Ancient Egyptian nobles hunted them, and representations of such hunts were sometimes included among the wall decorations of tombs. The method employed was to attach a cord to a barb and to project it by means of a harpoon. When several barbs had entered the animal so that it had become weak through loss of blood, it was pulled to the bank by the cords and killed. This figure, however, shows the king engaged not in an ordinary hippopotamus hunt but in the performance of a religious rite.

According to a legend preserved in a late text on a wall of the temple of Edfu, the god Re-Horakhty when he ruled on earth conducted a military expedition into Nubia accompanied by his son, Horus. While still away from home he received news that his throne was in danger and he decided to return to Egypt. On reaching Edfu he instructed Horus to attack the enemy, whose identity is not at that point specified, though subsequently reference is made to Seth and his confederates. Horus carried out his attack by first flying to the sky in the form of the sun's disk with wings and then swooping down on the enemy, killing very many, though a number seem to have escaped. Thinking that his victory was complete, he returned to the boat of Re-Horakhty. The surviving enemies, however, changed themselves into hippopotami and crocodiles in order to attack the sun-god in his boat. Once more the battle was taken up by Horus and this time he and his followers slaughtered the enemy with harpoons, pursuing them down the

Nile until they were utterly destroyed.

Although the legend – which is not the only one of its kind – had probably undergone many changes in detail by the time it was recorded at Edfu for presentation in the form of a drama, the essential features are unlikely to have been very different in the days of Tutankhamun. This figure very probably commemorates such an event, or at least another in the same cycle, with the king impersonating the god Horus, of whom he was thought to be the earthly embodiment. The hippopotamus of Seth, the god of evil, would not be shown for magical reasons because his presence might be a source of danger to the king.

Artistically this piece is an outstanding example of the Egyptian sculptor's ability to represent realistically the poise of the human body at a chosen point in course of movement.

FIGURE
Height 69.5 cm.
PEDESTAL
Length 70.5 cm, width 18.5 cm, height 5.6 cm.

Carter III: 54–6, pls XIII, LX; Desroches-Noblecourt pl XLV; Drioton 41, pl 120; Fairman 28–36; Fox pl 57; Riesterer pl 24; Vandier III: 358, pl CXV, 6.

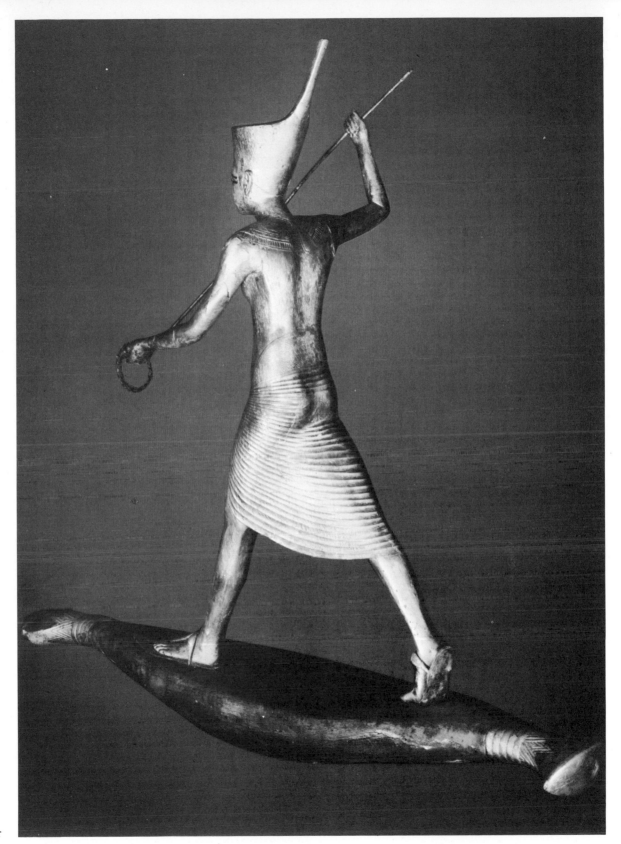

▷ Colour

Like the model of the king harpooning from a boat, this composite figure is one of a pair of images which were shrouded in linen sheets and placed in a single black wooden shrine against the south wall of the Treasury. Apart from details such as the uraeus and the sandals, both of which are made of gilded bronze, it is entirely carved of wood, the figure of the king being coated with gesso and gilded. The eyes and eyebrows are inlaid with glass. Only the facial markings and the internal pectinations of the ears of the leopard are gilded; the rest of the body is covered with a black resin varnish. The king's dress is the same as in the standing and the harpooning figures, except that he wears the white crown of Upper Egypt. The objects in his hands are all different. In this figure he has a flail in the right hand and a long staff in the left, his handrest being in the shape of a papyrus umbel. Both these objects are made of gilded bronze. The name of the king is painted in yellow on his pedestal.

The purpose of the figure remains unexplained and there is nothing in Egyptian mythology which sheds any light on its significance. Wooden leopards with mortises cut in their backs, which when complete must have been parts of similar models, were found in the tombs of Amenophis II (c 1450–1425 BC), Tuthmosis IV (c 1425–1417 BC) and Horemheb (c 1348–1320 BC), but, apart from showing that the Tutankhamun examples were not without parallel in the tomb equipment of kings in the Eighteenth Dynasty, they offer no help in solving the problem of

their interpretation. Rather more instructive is a painted representation of a figure of the same general character on a wall in the tomb of Sethos II (c 1216–1210 BC), the chief difference being that the statuette of the king and its pedestal are mounted upon a lion. From this slender evidence it may be deduced that such figures were connected with incidents in the passage of the king through the Underworld, but their nature is completely obscure.

Height 85.6 cm.
KING
Height 56.4 cm.
PEDESTAL OF KING
Length 24.6 cm, width 9.5 cm, height 4.8 cm.
LEOPARD
Height 19.4 cm.
PEDESTAL OF LEOPARD
Length 79.0 cm, width 14.0 cm, height 5.0 cm.

Carter III: 56, pl XIV; Desroches-Noblecourt 249, pl 158; Bonnet 581–2; Fox pl 56; Riesterer pl 24; Vandier III: 359, pl CXV 5.

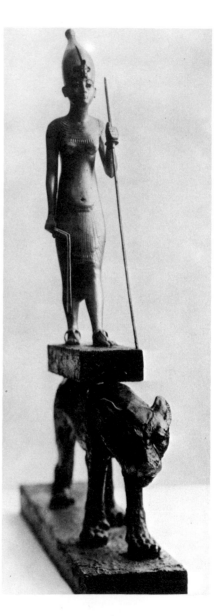

▷ Colour

A spell in the Book of the Dead (chapter 158) ends with the instruction that it is to be recited 'over a collar of gold inscribed with the spell and placed on the neck of the deceased on the day of burial'. The vignette which accompanies the spell represents a bead collar with falcon-head terminals. No single element in the painted decoration of mummiform coffins occurs so consistently as the broad bead collar, with or without the falcon-head terminals at the level of the shoulders. Most of the other decorative features were varied both in character and in arrangement according to the fashions of the time and, perhaps, the wishes of the purchasers, but the collar on the neck remained essentially un-changed with the utmost regularity. Tutankhamun's three mummiform coffins were no exception to the rule, and in addition seventeen actual collars were placed on his mummy within the linen bandages which covered his neck and chest. Some of these collars were com-posed of beads, but the majority were made of gold, either decorated with cloisonné work (see no 40) or plain with the details engraved.

Two examples of the plain type, both cut out of single sheets of gold, are displayed in this exhibition. One repro-duces a collar of five contiguous rows of upright cylindrical beads, laid side by side, and a lower border of beads imitating white lotus buds. At each end of the collar is a terminal bar, to which the suspensory strings are connected. A falcon head is mounted on the top of each bar. It is the distinguishing feature which signifies that the dead king was under the protection of the falcon-god Horus. The other collar represents the cobra-goddess Wadjet with wings of a falcon or a vulture. Wadjet was the tutelary goddess of the predynastic kings of Lower Egypt whose sanctuary lay at Buto (the Greek equivalent of the Egyptian name 'House of Wadjet') in the north-western Delta.

Both these collars were suspended from the neck by single strands of gold wire to which a small counterpoise *(mānkhet)*, also made of gold, was attached, so that it hung down from the nape of the neck.

Cobra collar, width 33.0 cm.
Falcon collar, width 29.0 cm.

Carter II: 120–22, pls XXX, LXXIXA, B; Wilkinson pl XXXV (falcon collar only); Japan Exh nos 11, 25; USA Exh no 14 (cobra collar only).

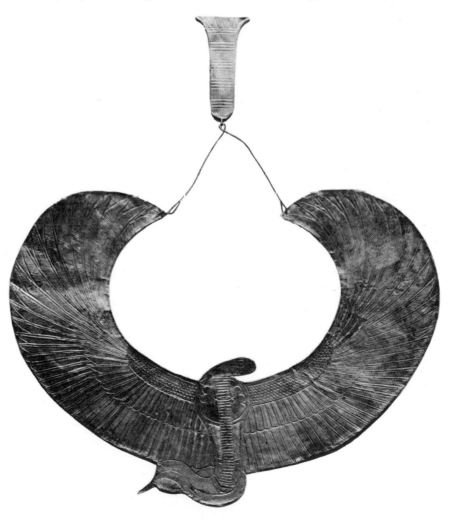

▷ See no 41 for picture of falcon collar

The central motif in this gold cloisonné pectoral is a scarab of translucent greenish-yellow chalcedony which serves as the body of a falcon with wings outstretched. It has the forelegs of a scarab and, at the back, falcon's legs of gold. In both talons it grasps the hieroglyphic sign for 'eternity' *(shen)* and in one an open lily, while the other holds a lotus-flower and buds. Bordering this motif on each side is a cobra with the sun's disk on its head and a long tail extending upwards to form an outer frame for the tops of the falcon-wings. A band of blue and red disks stretches from one cobra to the other beneath the winged scarab.

In Egyptian symbolism the sun-god could be represented both as a scarab (see no 34) and as a falcon. Composite forms of two related symbols were common in Egyptian iconography as a way of indicating two originally separate concep-tions which had been fused in the course of time. The designer of this pectoral, having produced a twofold symbol of the sun, repeated the technique, but less effectively, in the case of the moon. Above the winged scarab, supported by its front legs and the tips of its wings, is a gold bark, its hull inlaid in the centre with turquoise. That it is the bark of the moon is shown by the left 'Eye of Horus' which was one of the symbols of the moon, the right 'Eye of Horus' being a symbol of the sun. Two cobras with sun's disks flank the eye, perhaps as symbols of Upper and Lower Egypt, on both of which the moon shines. The eye alone would have been enough to indicate that the bark belonged to the

moon, but the artist has added to it the disk and crescent of the moon. The disk is appropriately made of silver and applied to its surface are small golden figures of the ibis-headed moon-god Thoth, the king and Re-Horakhty, the two former wearing the moon's disk and crescent and Re-Horakhty the sun's disk with uraeus.

As a kind of fringe at the base of the pectoral are the blue lotus-flowers, poppies, complex buds and papyrus flowers, all separated at the point where

the stem joins the flower or the bud by roundels of concentric circles.

This pectoral was found in the same casket as the necklace of the rising sun (no 32). It is inlaid with carnelian, lapis lazuli, calcite, obsidian (?), turquoise, red, blue, green, black and white glass.

Height 14.9 cm, width 14.5 cm.

Carter III: 76, pl XIXB; Desroches-Noblecourt pl XXXVI; Vilímková pl 36.

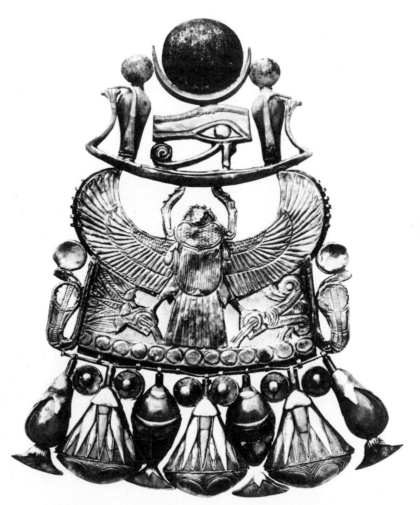

▷ Colour

Close to the necklace with a vulture-pectoral (no 43) in the wrappings of Tutankhamun's mummy lay a second necklace of a more elaborate design. Its rectangular gold pectoral is decorated with three upright scarabs inlaid with lapis lazuli, their front legs attached to the top of the frame, which is shaped like the hieroglyphic sign for 'heaven' *(pet)*. Engraved on its outer face is a row of stars. The sides of the frame are formed of two *was* sceptres and the base consists of a bar ornamented on the outer surface with twelve marguerites, the petals of which are made of dark blue glass and the centres of gold. Suspended from the bottom of the bar like a fringe are four blue lotus flowers, three large buds and three (originally six) small buds. The lotus flowers and the large buds are inlaid with carnelian, felspar and dark blue glass and the smaller buds with carnelian only. Above each scarab is a metal disk, the two outer disks of gold alloyed with copper representing the sun *(re)* and the centre disk with a crescent of gold alloyed with silver representing the moon. Beneath each scarab is the hieroglyphic sign for 'lord' *(neb)* inlaid with felspar. The gold undersides of the scarabs are finely modelled and the backs of the *neb* signs delicately chased. Contiguous circles of dark blue glass with gold centres take the place of the marguerites on the back of the base of the frame.

Egyptian jewellers often modified regular symbols or motifs for reasons which are not always apparent, though space and artistic effect were generally

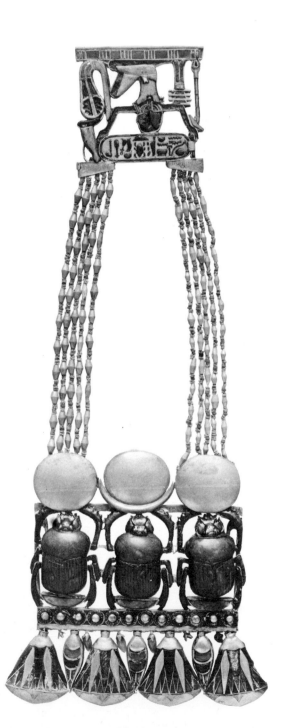

governing factors. In this pendant each
scarab group was probably intended to
suggest the name which Tutankhamun
adopted when he succeeded to the throne,
Nebkheperure, but the three vertical
strokes which should stand between the
beetle *(kheper)* and the basket *(neb)* (see
no 42) are missing. Also, in the middle
group, the sun's disk *(re)* is replaced by the
lunar disk and crescent. In hieroglyphic
writing it is possible to repeat the same
sign three times to indicate that a word is
in the plural, instead of adding the three
vertical strokes to the single sign, and thus
the three scarabs may, by allowing for
artistic licence, be explained as performing
the function. The word itself means the
different 'forms' *(kheperu)* which a god or
a dead person could assume, and it is
possible that the emphasis given by the
threefold repetition was intended to assist,
through the processes of magic, in the
realization of those metamorphoses. The
substitution of the lunar disk and
crescent for the sun's disk is a sportive
variant which is exemplified again in the
winged scarab pectoral no 42.

Five strings of gold beads, together
with a few beads of blue glass, make up the
straps – now shorter in length than they
were originally – on which the pectoral
was suspended from the king's neck.
A gold counterpoise inlaid with glass is
joined to the upper ends of the straps by
spacer-fastenings on which winged cobras
are engraved. In the centre of the counterpoise is a figure of the god of 'Millions of
Years', Ḥeḥ, squatting on a mat and
holding with raised arms a cartouche

bearing the inscription 'The Good God
Nebkheperure chosen of Amon-Re'. He is
supported on one side by the amuletic
signs for 'stability' *(djed)* and 'prosperity'
*(was)* and on the other side by the royal
cobra with the white crown of Upper
Egypt to which the curved frontal projection of the red crown of Lower Egypt has
been added.

PENDANT
Height 11.5 cm, width 9.0 cm.
CLASP
Height 5.0 cm, width 5.6 cm.

Carter II: 124–5, pl LXXXIVC; Wilkinson
pl LIII.

Among several pieces of jewellery which were not intended for funerary purposes was this unique necklace. It was found in the Treasury, together with some ornaments, in an oblong wooden casket overlaid with ivory and ebony. An ink inscription on the inside of the lid describes the contents of the casket as: 'Golden jewellery [?] belonging to the funerary procession made in the bed-chamber of Nebkheperure' (*ie* Tutankhamun), a description which is difficult to explain unless the bed-chamber was a synonym for the Burial Chamber. Like several other inscriptions of its kind, it was intended to help those who were packing the king's possessions to keep the various objects in their proper categories for the funeral procession and for storage in the tomb. Unfortunately the contents of the box suffered severely at the hands of the robbers and many of the links in the chain of this necklace have been lost.

The principal interest of this piece lies in the openwork pectoral-pendant of gold inlaid with semi-precious stones. Its central feature is a representation of the divine bark bearing the sun-god in the form of a gold scarab, encrusted with lapis lazuli, which supports the red disk of the sun with its forelegs (see no 34). Its hindlegs grasp the hieroglyphic sign for 'eternity' (*shen*). The bark is at the end of its nightly journey through the waters of the Underworld, shown as a band of lapis lazuli broken by wavy lines of gold. It is about to begin its daily journey across the sky, also represented in lapis lazuli but inlaid with fourteen stars of gold. At each

side of the pectoral, supporting the sky, is a gold *was* sceptre with a stylized head of an animal.

According to Egyptian mythology, the rising sun, as it emerged from the Underworld, was greeted by pairs of baboons, a concept which may have been suggested by the regular habit of baboons in nature of emitting shrieks at dawn. In this pectoral two baboons, seated on the tops of golden shrines, are shown, one on each side of the sun-god, their forepaws of lapis lazuli raised in adoration performing this daily ritual. On their heads, however, are the disks and crescents of the moon, which seem rather incongruous in this matutinal episode, although they are regularly added when baboons symbolize the moon-god Thoth. A text written on coffins (spell 156) some 500 years before the time of Tutankhamun refers to the crescent and disk in these words: 'That which is small on the second day of the (lunar) month and that which is large in the middle of the (lunar) month – it is Thoth'. The explanation in this instance may be that a conflation of ideas has taken place, Thoth being one of the gods who usually accompanied the sun-god in his bark. A further reason for the disks may be that the baboons alone would not have occupied the available space, and a gap between the heads and the sky-symbol would have been both inartistic and a source of structural weakness.

The necklace consists of twenty-two rectangular links bordered by small beads of gold and lapis lazuli. Each link embodies an amuletic motif. The two

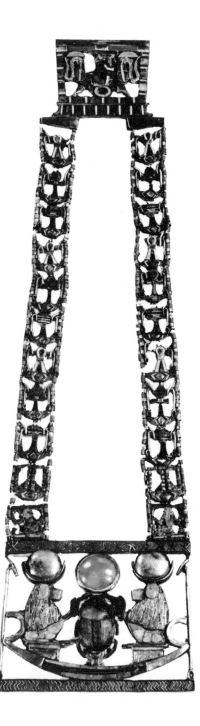

lowest links, which are attached to the pectoral, are composed of figures of the god of Millions of Years, Ḥeḥ, holding a palm-rib (the hieroglyph for 'year') in each hand and surmounted by the sky-sign. Above these links are two emblems of the royal jubilee festival consisting of a pair of thrones, back to back within pavilions, the whole mounted on the hieroglyph for 'festival'. All the remaining links also have as the base element the 'festival' sign supporting two *was* sceptres flanking the sign for 'stability' (*djed*), 'life' (*ānkh*) or 'protection' (*sa*).

At the upper end of the necklace is an elaborate shrine-shaped clasp. Within the shrine, seated on a green mat, is the anthropomorphic god Ḥeḥ holding above his head the hieroglyph for eternity instead of the usual palm-ribs. On the right side he is supported by a cobra wearing the crown of Upper Egypt and on the other side a cobra wearing the crown of Lower Egypt, both cobras being mounted on the 'basket' hieroglyph signifying 'lady'.

Length 41.0 cm. Maximum height of pectoral 8.6 cm, maximum width 10.8 cm. Maximum height of counterpoise 5.7 cm, maximum width 6.3 cm.

Riesterer 42, pl 42; Wilkinson 142, pl LII; Paris Exh no 21.

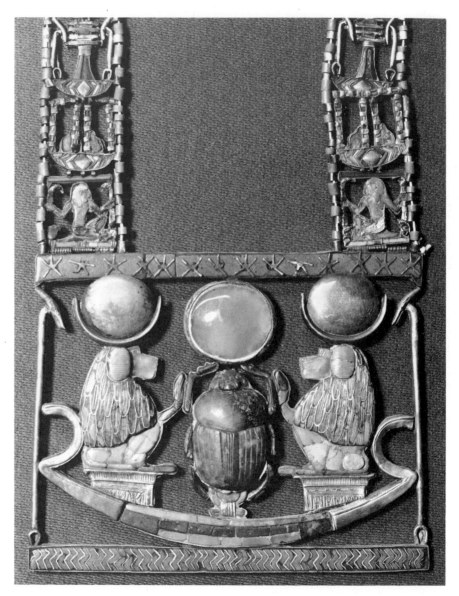

One of the most striking features of
Egyptian symbolism is the number of
different ways in which a single theme
could be pictorially expressed. Both this
necklace and the necklace of the rising
sun (no 32) commemorate in their inlaid
gold pectoral pendants what is essentially
the same daily event, but in this instance
the baboons are omitted. The baboons, by
their presence, showed that the action was
taking place at sunrise, whereas in this
case the same effect is produced by the use
of the hieroglyphic sign for 'horizon'
(*akhet*), which represents the sun rising
between two mountains. It involves the
introduction of a foreign element (*ie* the
mountains) into the naturalistic episode of
the scarab (= the sun-god) pushing its ball
of dung (= the sun) in front of it (see
no 34). By this slight deviation from what
was regular and normal, the artist has
given temporal and local precision to a
symbol which would otherwise have
lacked any indication of time and place.
He has also added uraei with pendent
'life' signs (*ānkh*) to the 'horizon' hieroglyph, thus signifying that the rising sun is
bringing life to Upper and Lower Egypt.

Apart from the symbol the sun-god's
gold bark bears two uraei, one in the prow
and the other in the stern, the head of each
uraeus surmounted by the disk of the sun
and the tail replaced by three amulets
symbolizing 'goodness' (*nefer*), 'life'
(*ānkh*) and 'stability' (*djed*). The straps are
composed of separate inlaid gold plaques
held together at the back and the sides by
rows of small gold, carnelian and glass
beads. The plaques embody the same

elements as those in the pectoral pendant,
except that the sun's disk is substituted for
the sign of the horizon and the hieroglyphic sign for 'festival' is placed beneath
the scarab. At the upper end of each strap
is a curved shoulder-piece representing the
vulture of the goddess Nekhbet with wings
outstretched. Two strings of beads join the
vultures to the clasp, which consists of a
pair of inlaid gold uraei with a slide-
fastening in the centre.

The semi-precious stones which form
the inlay of the various elements in this
piece are lapis lazuli, carnelian, felspar
and turquoise. It was found in the same
casket as the necklace of the rising sun
(no 32).

Length 50.0 cm.

Carter III: 76, pl XIXA; Desroches-
Noblecourt pl XXXVIII; Fox 28, pl 47;
Lange and Hirmer pl XL; Wilkinson 142,
pl LV.

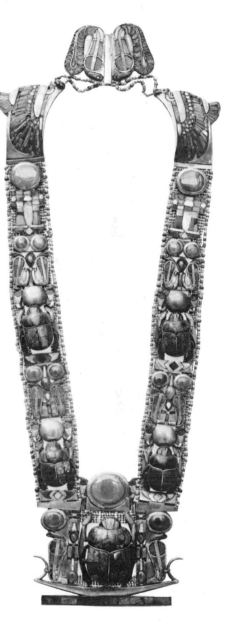

▷ Colour

Found with a quantity of jewellery, clothing and other personal possessions in a gilt chest stored in the Antechamber, this scarab is composed of several pieces of gold soldered together and its back is inlaid with blue glass. The tubular projections at the ends of the base suggest that it formed part of a large ornament, but its character is not evident.

The central figure on the embossed base represents Tutankhamun, whose name, Nebkheperure, is engraved in the cartouche above and to the right of his head preceded by the title 'Lord of the Two Lands' (*ie* Upper and Lower Egypt). He wears the so-called *atef* crown with ram's horns and uraei, the heads of which bear disks of the sun, and the striped royal headdress (*nemes*) with uraeus. A corselet covers his shoulders and the upper part of his chest. A pointed kilt with apron and an animal's tail, suspended from the back of the girdle of the apron, complete his attire. Two gods, Atum and Re-Horakhty, stand one on each side of him holding his hands, and they also are shown with pendent tails like the king's. Re-Horakhty, with falcon's head surmounted by the sun's disk and uraeus, extends, with his left hand, the symbol of 'life' (*ānkh*) to the nostrils of the king. He is described in the accompanying inscription as 'Re-Horakhty, the god who is in Heliopolis, lord of heaven and lord of the Two Lands'. Atum, in the corresponding inscription on the other side of the king, is called 'Atum, lord of the Two Lands of Heliopolis, great god, lord of heaven and lord of the Two Lands'. Above the king's crown is the sun's disk, flanked

by uraei; at its base are seven pendent 'life' symbols, relics of the Amarna custom of terminating the sun's rays with these symbols.

In a separate compartment, beneath the feet of the three figures, is a design composed of two identical antithetical groups facing the hieroglyphic symbol for unity (*sma*) supported by intertwined lotus and papyrus stems and flowers, emblems of Upper and Lower Egypt (see no 3). Each of the antithetical groups has as its principal element a lapwing (*Vanellus cristatus*) with human arms and hands projecting from its chest and extending towards the symbol of unity. Beneath the arms are a five-pointed star and a basket which serves as a perch for the feet of the bird. The lapwing, the star and the basket are all hieroglyphic signs and their respective meanings are 'people' (*rekhyt*), 'adore' (*dwa*), and 'all' (*neb*). In combination with the sign for unity they may be translated: 'Adoration by all people of the unification of Upper and Lower Egypt'.

The ancient Egyptians adopted the scarab (*Ateuchus sacer*) as a symbol of the sun-god because they were familiar with the sight of the beetle rolling a ball of dung on the ground and this action suggested to them that the invisible power which rolled the sun daily across the sky could be represented pictorially as a scarab. Moreover, they had noticed that the young beetle emerged from a ball of dung by what they imagined to be an autogenic process, so that a further parallel was seen between this creature and the sun-god, who was also credited with having created

himself. In reality the ball of dung rolled by the scarab is only a reserve supply of food which it hides in a convenient crevice, whereas the ball containing the egg is pear-shaped and is never moved from the burrow in which it is placed by the female. In the Egyptian language the words for the scarab and for existence were identical (*kheper*), and the name of the sun-god, on his first appearance every morning (see nos 32 and 33), was Khepri. In hieroglyphic writing the scarab sign was used for all three words.

Length 5.2 cm, width 3.9 cm.

Carter I: 114, pl LXVA; USA Exh no 6; Japan Exh no 5.

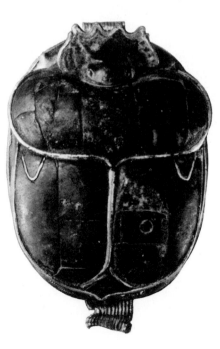

Of the many pieces of jewellery found in the tomb of Tutankhamun certainly one of the richest was this massive gold bracelet. It was stored in the same cartouche-shaped box as the earrings (no 39) shown in this exhibition, and this circumstance alone would suggest that it was a personal possession, worn by the king in his lifetime, and not an object specially made for sepulchral purposes. Moreover, its small size indicates that its manufacture dated from his childhood.

The central feature is a gold openwork scarab encrusted with lapis lazuli. On each side is a narrow raised band composed of gold, lapis lazuli, turquoise, quartz and carnelian inlay, bordered on the inner edge with gold granules. The bands are continued on the back of the hoop. Two identical botanical ornaments flank the scarab, each consisting of a mandrake fruit supported by two floral buds, with gold rosettes filling the interstices between the stems of the mandrake and the buds. The yellow and green colours of the mandrakes are painted at the back of the translucent quartz inlay. Buds with red ovoid petals and golden sepals, similar in shape to those in this floral composition, are depicted on each side of two papyrus flowers on the lid of a painted alabaster box inscribed with the names of Tutankhamun and his queen (no 5). In this bracelet the petals are inlaid with red carnelian. They are believed to represent poppies. Both the hinge and the fastening are made of interlocking cylindrical teeth held together by long gold pins, the hinge-pin being fixed and the other movable.

In spite of black being the colour of the scarab in nature, the Egyptians seldom copied it in their reproductions, perhaps because there was no native semi-precious stone of that colour, and obsidian, volcanic glass, was not easily obtainable. Quite exceptionally two scarabs placed on Tutankhamun's mummy were made of black resin. Glazed specimens were usually green or light blue, and it is clear that no importance was attached to reproducing an exact likeness of the living beetle. Lapis lazuli, the material used for most of the scarabs in Tutankhamun's collection of jewellery, has not been found in Egypt, the nearest source at present known being Badakhshan in the north-east of Afghanistan.

Maximum diameter 5.4 cm.

Carter III: 77, pl XXA; Fox 28, pl 48B; Vilímková pl 54; Wilkinson pl XXX.

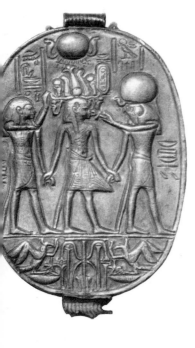

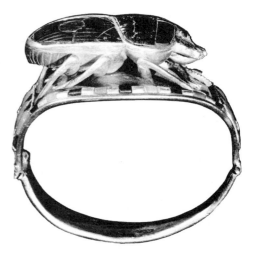

▷ Colour

Daggers were used by the ancient Egyptians from predynastic times onwards, though examples dating from the Old Kingdom (c 2700–2180 BC) are exceedingly rare. During the Middle Kingdom (c 2100–1700 BC) and the New Kingdom (c 1570–1000 BC) they were generally made of copper or bronze; gold, apart from its use for purposes of embellishment, was probably reserved for royalty. Queen Ahhotpe, mother of Ahmosis I, the founder of the Eighteenth Dynasty, had, in her funerary equipment, a solid gold dagger and sheath, both of which are now in the Cairo Museum. Tutankhamun's mummy was provided with two daggers encased in gold sheaths, one with an iron blade and the other with a blade of hardened gold. It is the latter specimen which is shown here.

As an illustration of the goldsmith's artistic ability and technical skill, this dagger, and particularly its sheath, are among the outstanding pieces of the collection. On the top of the pommel are the king's cartouches in applied embossed gold and a wreath of lily-palmettes in

cloisonné work. On the underside are two figures of falcons holding in each claw the hieroglyphic symbol for 'eternity' (shen). The falcon was often represented in Egyptian art holding this symbol and, with wings outstretched, protecting a king. Probably it was intended to serve an amuletic purpose in this instance also. A similar motif appears on the haft of a dagger in the Metropolitan Museum which bears the name of Tuthmosis I (c 1525–1512 BC) and it may have been a characteristic feature of royal daggers at this period. Below the pommel, the haft is decorated with alternate bands of geometric designs in granulated gold work and lily palmette designs in gold cloisonné work of semi-precious stones and glass, a central band of minute red and blue circular disks breaking the regularity of the palmette ornamentation. At the base of the hilt, applied in gold wire, is a band of continuous spirals within a rope-pattern border, thus conveying to the eye the suggestion that the haft is bound to the blade.

In striking contrast with the ornate haft, the decoration of the blade, which is tinged with red, is simple. At the top, incised on both faces, is a plain horizontal band, which also suggests a tie, over a design consisting of a diamond-pattern chain bordered beneath by two horizontal lines, the spaces between the diamonds being filled with dots. Under this frieze is engraved an elegant palmette with poppies surmounting two perpendicular grooves which converge at the base and resemble floral stems.

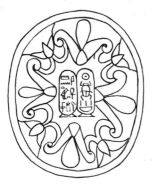

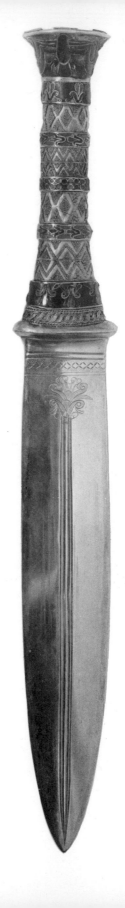

▷ Colour

The obverse of the gold sheath is almost entirely covered with a feather pattern decoration in cloisonné work, relieved at the top by a palmette frieze and at the pointed base by a jackal's head. Of far greater interest is the elaborate design on the reverse. First comes a line of inscription reading: 'The Good God, possessor of a strong arm, Nebkheperure, given life'. A row of continuous spirals follows and then two loops of palmette design, by means of which the sheath was attached to the girdle. The main scene, embossed in high relief, is composed of the following elements: an ibex attacked by a lion, a calf with a hound on its back biting the calf's tail, a leopard and a lion attacking a male ibex from above and below, a hound biting a bull, and lastly a calf in full flight. Interspersed between the animals are stylized plants, and a more elaborate floral device occupies the pointed base.

Although there is no reason to doubt that this sheath was made in Egypt, the decoration of the reverse includes artistic features which have a foreign appearance. The band of continuous spirals, the style of the rosette on the shoulder of the second lion (see no 37), the summary treatment of the skins of the animals and the floral motif at the base have parallels in the art of northern Syria at this period and they also have Minoan or Mycenaean affinities. Scenes of workshops painted on the walls of private tombs at Thebes sometimes include Asiatic craftsmen at work side by side with the far more numerous Egyptian artisans; they were very probably employed on account of their ability to

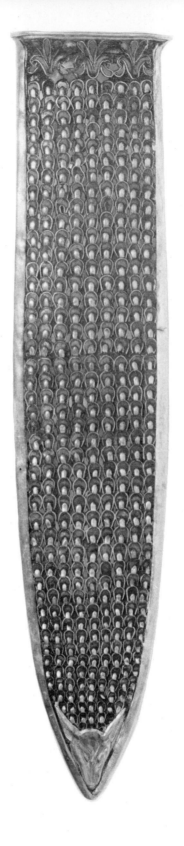
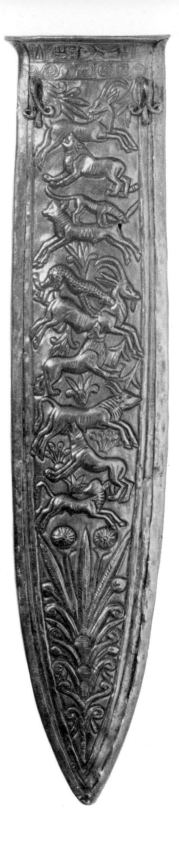

reproduce artistic styles which were
familiar to them but new to the Egyptians.
Like so many other importations in the
history of Egypt, however, these innovations were quickly absorbed and given
the general character of native products.

DAGGER
Length 31.9 cm, blade 20.1 cm.
SHEATH
Length 21.0 cm, width 4.4 cm.

Carter II: 16, 131–2, pls LXXXVIIA,
LXXXVIIIA, B; Desroches-Noblecourt
232–3, pl XXIA, B; Drioton 42, pl 132;
Fox pl 37; Gardiner frontispiece;
Schaeffer 33–4; Paris Exh no 19;
Japan Exh no 1; USA Exh no 1.

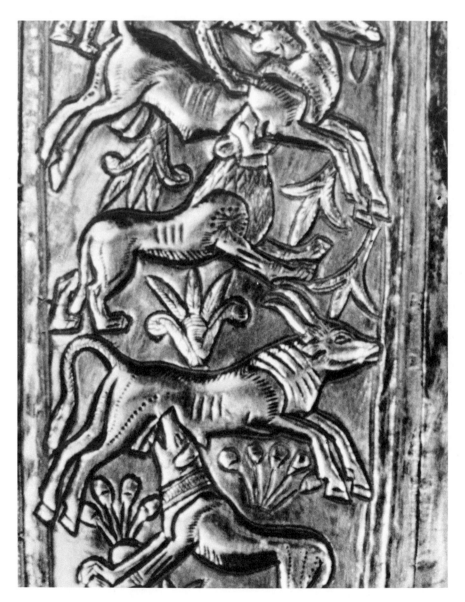

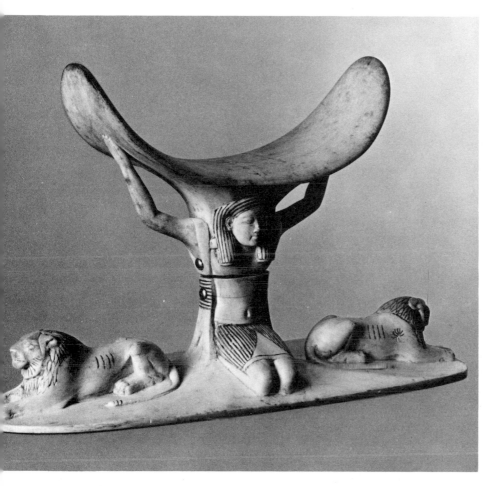

Egyptian head-rests show many variations in material, and in form they range from the plain to the elaborate. Usually they consist of three parts: a flat base, a small central pillar, and a curved support on which the head rested. In this ivory example, which has no close parallel in Egyptian art, the central pillar is formed mainly of a figure of the god Shu kneeling and holding with upraised arms the curved head-support. Looped over each of his shoulders is the hieroglyphic sign for 'protection'. Two couchant lions, carved almost in the round, are attached to the top of the base.

Shu was the god of the air and consequently his image was used as its symbol. According to legend he brought chaos to an end, at the creation of the universe, by raising the sky (symbolized by his daughter Nut) high above the earth (symbolized by his son Geb). It was an action which needed to be maintained continuously; failure to do so would result in the fall of the sky and a return to chaos.

The Egyptians regarded the head as the seat of life and consequently its preservation was thought to be of particular importance for continued existence after death. It could not, however, function without the help of magic which could be obtained by various means, one of which was an amulet in the form of a head-rest, either model or actual. Tutankhamun possessed four full-size head-rests and one model which was made of iron and was placed in the linen wrappings of his mummy at the back of the head – the natural position for such an object. A spell in the Book of the Dead (no 166) has been interpreted as attributing to the head-rest the power of resurrection, and another spell (no 55) which is sometimes written on head-rests actually identifies these objects with the god Shu, probably because air was a vital necessity for life.

In order to show symbolically that the base of the head-rest represents the earth or its god Geb, the artist has carved the two lions, one at each end of the base, representing the two mountains on the eastern and the western horizons between which the sun rose and set. As a development from this conception, two squatting lions placed back to back became a symbol for yesterday and tomorrow. On the shoulders of each lion is a kind of rosette, the interpretation of which is uncertain. It has been variously explained as representing a tuft of hair and an ornament placed on live lions at the court of a king. Its occurrence as an artistic feature is not confined to Egypt; it is also found in the art of Syria, Mesopotamia and Persia. The position of the tail, lying by the side of the body, is a peculiarity of the period. At other times it was curled over the flank.

Behind the figure of Shu is the hieroglyphic inscription: 'The Good God, son of Amun, king of Upper and Lower Egypt, lord of the Two Lands, Nebkheperure (*ie* Tutankhamun), given life like Re for ever'.

The object is made of two pieces of ivory joined by a wooden dowel in the middle of the figure of Shu and held together by four gold nails. Details of the sculpture are inlaid with a blue pigment. It was found, together with the three other headrests, in the wooden cabinet shown in the exhibition (no 15) which stood in the Annexe of the tomb.

Height 17.5 cm, length 29.1 cm, width 9.0 cm.

Carter III: 116–7, pl XXXVIB; Desroches-Noblecourt 288, fig 187; Fox pl 62; Paris Exh no 41.

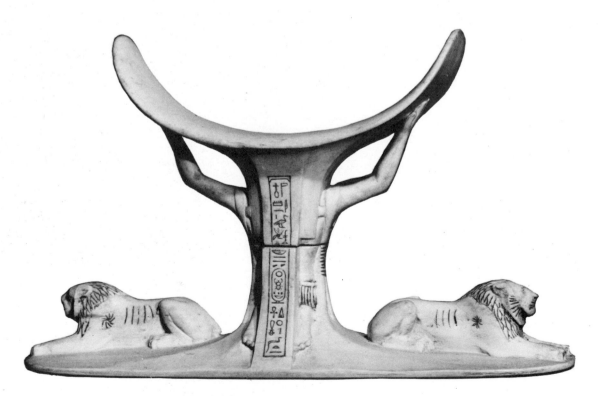

This sceptre is made of sheet-gold beaten on a wooden core. The shaft is in the form of a papyrus flower and stem; it is embellished at each end with a feather design in cloisonné work inlaid with carnelian, turquoise, lapis lazuli, felspar, faience and glass. Embossed on one side of the blade are rows of trussed and slaughtered bulls, partly dismembered, beneath a frieze of lotus petals between borders of chequer and diamond patterns. On the other side of the blade, beneath a similar frieze, is an inscription which reads: 'The Good God, the beloved, dazzling of face like the Aten when it shines, the son of Amun Nebkheperure, living for ever'.

Sceptres of this kind have three names in Egyptian texts, *kherep* 'the controller', *sekhem* 'the powerful' and *āba* 'the commander'. They were carried as symbols of authority from very early times, but no distinction can be drawn between their various uses. In temple ritual and in the mortuary service the *āba* sceptre was often held by the officiant who presented the offerings. If the sacrificial offerings shown on the blade of this sceptre are indicative of its use, it probably represents the *āba* sceptre, but precise identification is not possible. It was found in the Annexe whither it had probably been taken from the Treasury by the robbers.

Length 54.0 cm, width 6.6 cm.

Carter III: 133–4, pl XLIV; Desroches-Noblecourt 202, pl 122; Fox 33, pl 67.

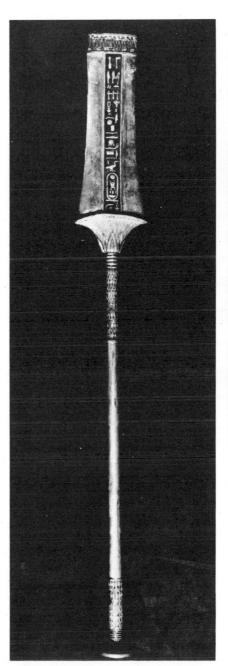
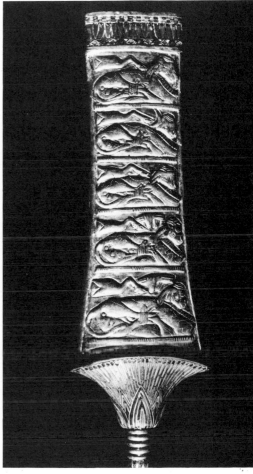

A cartouche-shaped wooden box found in the Treasury contained, among other pieces of jewellery, this remarkable pair of gold earrings. In order to attach them to the pierced lobes of the ears, a studlike clasp was made in two pieces so that it could be taken apart. Each piece is composed of a short cylindrical tube closed at one end by a gold disk with raised rim, on which is mounted a hemispherical button of transparent quartz. When the clasp is closed, one tube fits inside the other. A portrait of the king is painted behind one button on each earring, the painting being visible through the quartz covering. Two pendent uraei attached to the disks flank the portraits. Suspended on ring-eyelets from the clasps are figures of hybrid birds with gold cloisonné bodies and wings of falcons and heads of ducks. The wings are curved inwards so that they meet at the top to form a complete circle. In their claws the birds hold the hieroglyphic sign for 'eternity' (*shen*). The heads are made of translucent blue glass and the bodies and wings are inlaid with quartz, calcite, coloured faience and blue, red, white and green glass. Pendent extensions from the tails of the birds consist of openwork gold frames encrusted with alternate rows of gold and blue inlay, arranged in a feather pattern, and cylindrical blue and gold beads which terminate in five heads and hoods of uraei.

Earrings were a relatively recent innovation at the time of Tutankhamun. They were probably a legacy of the Hyksos invaders who brought them from Western Asia, where they had been in vogue for many centuries. The earliest recorded examples in Egypt were found by Sir Flinders Petrie in a tomb at Thebes which he dated to the end of the Seventeenth Dynasty (*c* 1570 BC). At first they seem to have been worn chiefly by women, not merely by members of the nobility but also by some of those who served the nobility, such as muscians and dancers (*cf* the tomb paintings of banqueting scenes exhibited in the Third Egyptian Room of the Museum which date from the reign of Tuthmosis III, *c* 1504–1450 BC). According to one of the Amarna letters, earrings were among the principal items of jewellery brought by a Mitannian princess to Egypt at the time of her marriage to Amenophis III (*c* 1417–1379 BC). How soon, and to what extent, the custom was adopted by men is uncertain, but the first king whose mummy shows pierced lobes of the ears is Tuthmosis IV (*c* 1425–1417 BC). Perhaps it is no more than a coincidence that he was the first Egyptian king to marry a Mitannian princess, because instances of men wearing earrings occur in the wall paintings of at least two Theban tombs which antedate his reign. Compared, however, with the countless representations of female wearers of earrings, the number of representations of male wearers is very small and, in the main, confined to young princes. Nevertheless the lobes of the ears of the mummies of several kings, including Sethos I (c 1318–1304 BC) and Ramesses II (c 1304–1237 BC), were pierced and it must be supposed that at some stage in their lives they wore earrings. Moreover, sculptures of kings from Amenophis III to Ramesses II often show pierced lobes. A possible explanation is that earrings were normally – though not invariably, and particularly not in Amarna times – discarded by boys when they reached manhood. Such an explanation would accord with the fact that, in spite of the profusion of other kinds of jewellery, no earrings were placed on the mummy of Tutankhamun. It would also account for the covering with gold foil of the perforations in the ears of the gold mask (see no 50). That these earrings were actually used by Tutankhamun is highly probable, because they show signs of friction.

Length 10.9 cm, width 5.2 cm.

Carter III: 74–5, pl XVIII; Drioton 42, pl 130; Fox pl 49A; Möller 38–45; Riesterer pl 40; Wilkinson pl XLVB; Paris Exh no 16.

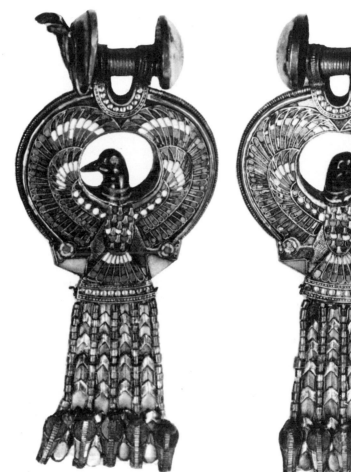

This flexible gold collar, in the form of the vulture of the goddess Nekhbet (see no 43), was placed on the thorax of the king's mummy so that it covered the whole of the chest and extended upwards to the shoulders. The elongated wings, set in a circular fashion, are divided into 'districts'. They are composed of 250 segments, engraved on the back and inlaid on the front with 'feathers' of polychrome glass in imitation of turquoise, jasper and lapis lazuli. The segments were held together by thread which passed through small golden eyelets projecting from the upper and lower edges. On one side-margin of each segment, except in the 'district' known as the lesser coverts, there is a border of minute gold beads which divides its 'feathers' from those of its neighbour. The body of the bird is inlaid in the same manner as the lesser coverts, while the tail-feathers resemble the primary and the secondary 'districts' of the wings. Both the beak and the eye in the delicately chased head are made of obsidian. In each of the talons the bird grasps the hieroglyphic sign for 'eternity' (*shen*) inlaid with red and blue glass. A floral-shaped counterpoise (*mānkhet*), which was attached by gold wires to eyelets at the back of the wings, hung down the back of the mummy.

Collars and necklaces were placed on Egyptian mummies not as objects of adornment but to provide magical protection. They were also represented on the cartonnage covers of mummies and on the lids of anthropoid coffins. Among the many collar-amulets painted on the walls of rectangular wooden coffins dating from the Eleventh Dynasty (*c* 2000 BC) are four made of gold and inlaid on the outer surface, shaped to represent a falcon, a vulture, a winged cobra and a combined vulture and cobra. Tutankhamun's mummy, which was more than half a millennium later in date than these coffins, was equipped with all these inlaid collars except the cobra-collar, and also with all four collars in sheet gold without inlay (see nos 29 and 41). They were purely funerary in character and very different from the bead or gold collars worn in life.

Height 39.5 cm, width 48.0 cm.

Carter II: 123–4, pl LXXXB; Vilímková pl 45; Wilkinson pl XXXVIA; Paris Exh no 20.

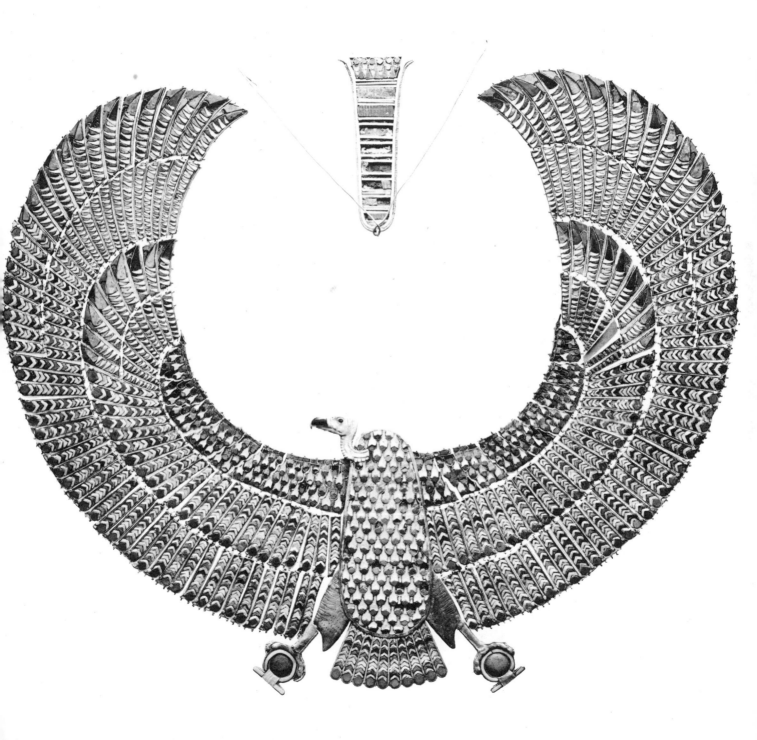

▷ See no 29 for description

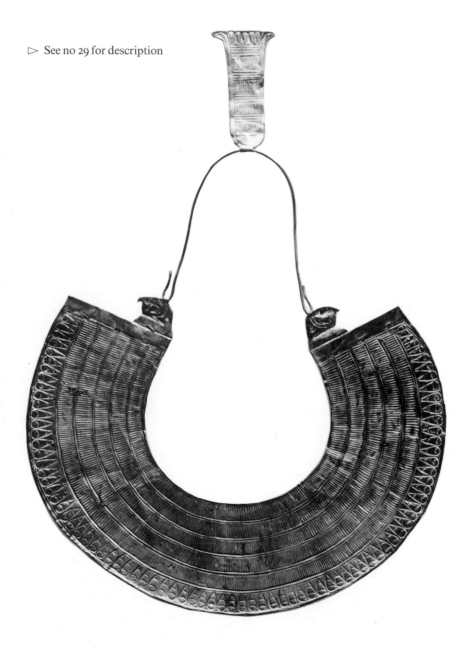

Concealed beneath the twelfth layer of the
linen bandages which enveloped the king's
mummy were three necklaces with
pendant-pectorals, one lying over the
centre of the thorax and the others
supporting it on the left and right sides.
The middle pectoral bore the Eye of Horus
flanked by a vulture and a cobra, the
pectoral over the right side of the body
was in the form of a falcon with wings
curved upwards and a solar disk with
uraeus on its head, and the third pectoral
was the one shown here. It represents a
winged scarab holding in its forelegs the
lunar disk and crescent and in its backlegs
the basin. Between the scarab and the
basin, attached to each of them, are three
gold bars. The whole piece is made of solid
gold decorated on the outer surface with
cloisonné work of lapis lazuli, carnelian
and turquoise-coloured glass. In the lunar
disk alone the gold is alloyed with silver.
All the details of the elements in its
composition are finely engraved in the
gold base on the inner surface.

It is evident that the pectoral represents
the throne-name of Tutankhamun,
Nebkheperure, but two of its elements are
not the regular hieroglyphic signs used for
writing the name. The basin (*ḥeb*) has been
substituted for the basket (*neb*) and the
lunar disk and crescent (*īāḥ*) for the sun's
disk (*re*). In both cases the substitutions
can be explained as examples of artist's
licence (see no 31), but the basin may have
been intended to suggest the idea that the
king would live to celebrate many festivals
(*ḥeb*). Carter thought that the moon's disk
was intended to counterbalance the sun's

disk of the falcon necklace on the opposite
side of the central pectoral. He remarks,
however, that all these pectorals showed
signs of friction and it seems unlikely that
they would have been worn as a pair by the
king during his lifetime, though he may
well have worn them individually.

Chains of plaited gold wire connect the
pectoral with two inlaid gold lotus flowers
and a heart-shaped pendant separated by
two carnelian beads. The pendant is inlaid
with a cartouche bearing the king's name
written in the normal manner and two
uraei, one on each side of the cartouche.
Since the lotus flowers have five holes and
the pectoral is provided with a similar
number of eyelets at the tops of the wings,
it is probable that the suspensory chains
were originally intended to consist of five
strands of gold beads, like the chains of
necklace no 31.

Height of pectoral 9.0 cm, width 9.5 cm.

Carter II: 126–7, pl LXXXIVB; Riesterer
pl 46; Vilímková pls 38, 39.

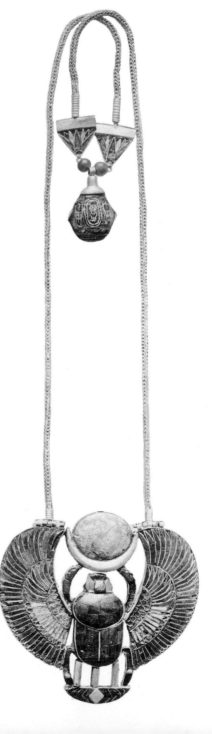

Tutankhamun's mummy was bandaged in layers, the appropriate amulets and jewellery being placed in each layer so that the innermost layers contained his personal possessions. This necklace was suspended from his neck between the eleventh or the twelfth layer, close to the mummy, and therefore very probably it was a piece which he had worn during his lifetime. The pendant consists of a representation of the vulture-goddess of Upper Egypt, Nekhbet, with the outer ends of the wings folded downwards resembling a cloak. It is made of solid gold encrusted, on the obverse, with lapis lazuli, apart from the lesser coverts of the wings, which are encrusted with carnelian edged with green glass, and the tips of the tail feathers, which are also encrusted with carnelian. In its talons it holds the hieroglyphic sign for 'eternity' (*shen*), inlaid with carnelian and blue glass. The gold head, turned sideways, and the neck are delicately rendered in a most realistic manner, the effect being heightened by the wrinkled occiput, the obsidian eyes and the lapis lazuli beak. On the chased reverse, a miniature necklace and pendant are modelled in high relief. The pendant is composed of the king's cartouche sur-mounted by the sun's disk and ostrich plumes, flanked by two uraei. Fastenings for the suspensory chains are attached to the upper edges of the wings. The chains are formed of rectangular links of gold and lapis lazuli inlaid, on the obverse, with concentric circles of coloured glass and bordered on the outer sides with minute gold and glass beads. Some of the lapis lazuli links had decayed before the necklace was found. The clasp consists of two falcons with heads turned backwards and resting on their scapules. Made of gold encrusted with lapis lazuli, felspar,

onyx, carnelian and green glass, they are connected by a gold tenon on the inner side of one bird which slides into a gold mortise on the inner side of the other bird.

Nekhbet, whose name means 'She who belongs to Nekheb', was originally simply the local goddess of Nekheb, the modern Elkab on the east bank of the Nile about halfway between Luxor and Aswan. She owed her importance in dynastic times to her previous adoption by the predynastic kings of Upper Egypt, whose seat lay at Nekhen (Hierakonpolis) across the river from Nekheb. According to tradition, the last of these kings, Menes, completed the conquest of Lower Egypt, the patron deity of whose kings was the cobra-goddess Wadjet, and united the two kingdoms under his sovereignty. The vulture and the cobra thus became the symbols of this unification and also the tutelary deities of the kings. Their heads were often placed side by side on the front of the headdresses worn by kings on state occasions, and on the headdresses of their statues and other representations. Frequently the entire cobra was reproduced in this setting, and they were also depicted singly, as the vulture in this pendant. It is said that this species of vulture (*Gyps fulvus*) has its habitat at the present day in Middle and Upper Egypt and farther south, but is seldom seen in Lower Egypt.

PENDANT
Maximum height 6.5 cm, maximum width 11.0 cm.

Carter II: 124, pl LXXXIVA; Desroches-Noblecourt 229–31, pl XXXVIIA; Drioton 42, pl 131; Fox pl 36; Lange and Hirmer pl XLI; Nims fig 31; Paris Exh no 18.

▷ Colour

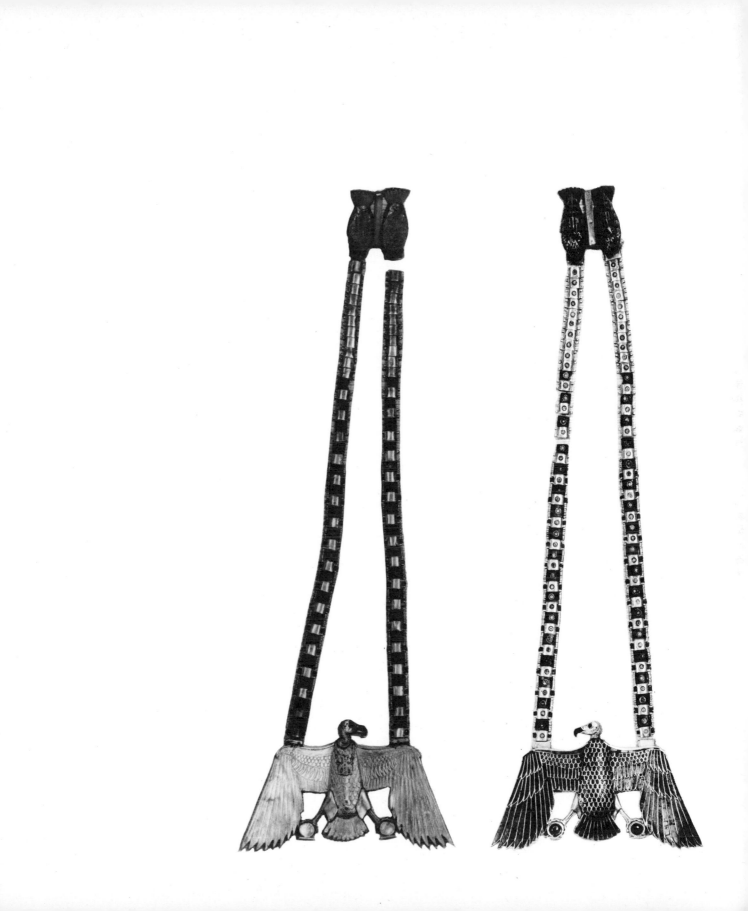

These emblems were found separately, the crook in the Antechamber and the flail in the Treasury. The flail is historically the more interesting because it bears on the gold cap at the base of its handle the king's name in its early form of Tutankhaten, together with his throne-name Nebkheperure, thus showing that it had belonged to him while he was still a child but after he had ascended the throne. Since a flail was one of the symbols held by Egyptian kings in some of their coronation ceremonies, it is at least possible that this object was the actual flail used by Tutankhaten in his coronation at El-Amarna when he was about nine years of age and before he was crowned at Karnak. The crook is inscribed on both the terminal caps with the throne-name only – a difference which, in spite of the equality in size of the two objects, may indicate that they were not originally made as a pair. A second pair and an odd crook, all of larger size, were found in the same wooden box as this flail. All three crooks are composed of alternating cylindrical sleeves of metal overlaid with gold and dark blue glass upon a bronze core. The handle of the flail, as far as the angular sleeve at the top, is similarly composed, but the gilded beads in the thongs of the swingle have wooden cores.

Although the crook and the flail were most often represented as emblems of the god Osiris, they were also carried on some ceremonial occasions, besides the coronation, by the reigning Pharaoh. Very occasionally the crook was held by Viceroys of Nubia and also by Viziers. A painted scene of tribute from Asia in the tomb of Tutankhamun's Viceroy of Nubia, Huy, shows the king holding both the crook and flail in his left hand and the sign for 'life' (*ānkh*) in his right, while the Viceroy holds a crook, but no flail, in his left hand and a single ostrich plume (see no 23) in his right. Only rarely is the flail shown in the hands of priests or officials and such instances are limited to scenes of royal jubilee festivals. Notwithstanding these sporadic exceptions, the crook and the flail were essentially Osirian emblems, though possibly not so in origin. Osiris is believed to have acquired them from Andjeti, the local god of a town in the Delta named Djedu, who was represented in human form with two feathers on his head and holding the crook and flail in his hands. At a very early date in Egyptian history Osiris absorbed Andjeti and adopted his insignia. Osiris, however, was regarded not only as a god but also as a deified deceased king and consequently his insignia, particularly the crook and the flail, were treated as symbols of royalty.

It is not difficult to imagine how a shepherd's crook could have acquired the symbolical significance of rulership. Its name in Egyptian is *ḥeqat* and the most common word for 'ruler' is *ḥeqa*. Not unnaturally it has been compared with the crozier, the pastoral staff of ecclesiastical appurtenances. A flail (called *nekhakha*), however, seems out of character for a kindly and beneficent god like Osiris and for this reason some authorities prefer to regard it as a *ladanisterion*, a flail-like instrument used until the present day by shepherds in the Mediterranean region and elsewhere for collecting ladanum, a gummy substance excreted from the leaves of the cistus plant. According to classical writers it was used in the preparation of incense and unguents. This suggestion, which was proposed by Professor P. E. Newberry who helped in the clearance of Tutankhamun's tomb, is plausible, but, as yet, there is no clear evidence that the cistus plant grew in Egypt in pharaonic times.

Length of crook (?) 33.5 cm.
Length of flail 33.5 cm.

Carter I: pl XXIIIA; III: 77–8, pl XXIA; Desroches-Noblecourt 86, 179, fig 104; Newberry 84–94; Paris Exh no 17; USA Exh nos 4–5; Japan Exh nos 3–4.

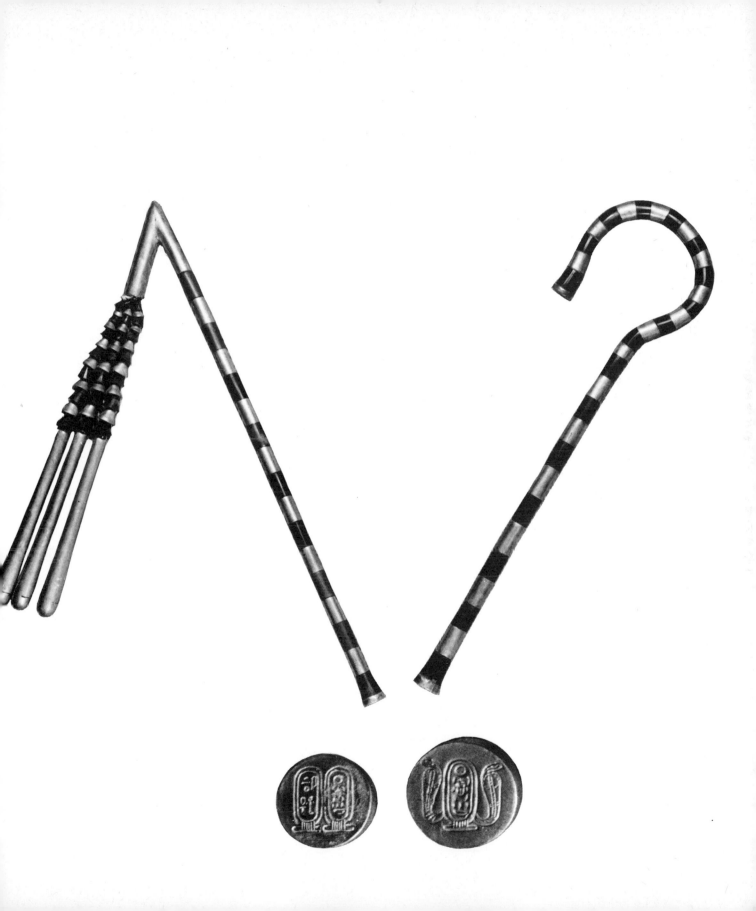

This trumpet, made of bronze or copper with gold overlay, is one of three known examples of the instrument preserved from ancient Egypt, two of which were found in the tomb of Tutankhamun; the third is in the Louvre. The bell is decorated with incised figures of the king and of three gods, all standing under the hieroglyphic sign for heaven: Re-Horakhty (falcon-headed), Amon-Re and Ptah (mummified within a shrine and holding three sceptres). With the trumpet is a wooden stopper to fit the tube and bell, almost certainly either for use with a cloth as a cleaner or to prevent the instrument being damaged and thus losing its shape when not in use. A hole at the thinner end of the stopper was probably intended for a thong by which it could be suspended beneath the arm from the shoulder while the trumpet was being blown. The bell is painted to resemble a lotus flower.

In comparison with a modern trumpet, this instrument is short and it has no valves. The mouthpiece is a cylindrical sleeve with a silver ring at the outer end fixed to the outside of the tube; it is not cup-shaped or detachable. Both this trumpet and its companion in the tomb, which is made of silver, have been played in recent times and the lowest notes which could be clearly sounded on them were D and C respectively. Plutarch (*De Iside et Osiride* 30) remarked that the people of Busiris and Lycopolis did not use trumpets because they sounded like the braying of an ass, the ass being identified with the god Seth, the murderer of Osiris. It has been stated (H. Hickman, *La trompette dans l'Egypte ancienne*, p 1) that the trumpet is the only ancient instrument of which the exact sound, as heard by the ancients, can be reproduced today.

Several scenes in tombs and temples illustrate the trumpet in use and in most instances it is associated with military activities – processions of soldiers, battle scenes, etc. A trumpeter and a standard-bearer are shown among the first Egyptian soldiers to scale the walls of an Asiatic town in a famous battle scene in the temple of Ramesses III at Medinet Habu (Western Thebes). Sometimes a pair of trumpeters is shown, but it is noticeable that they are never represented both playing at the same time. As a rule when he accompanied soldiers, the trumpeter marched outside the column punctuating by staccato notes the step of the soldiers.

Whether Tutankhamun's trumpets were intended solely for military purposes it is impossible to be certain. Nevertheless the figures of the gods on the bell would suggest such a use, for these three gods were the tutelary deities of three out of the four divisions of the army of Ramesses II at the battle of Qadesh (*c* 1300 BC), only about fifty years after the death of Tutankhamun. Their names and epithets are written in hieroglyphs above their figures. The king's name is also given. On his head he wears the blue crown (*khepresh*), while in his left hand he holds a *heqat* sceptre, of the same kind as no 44, and the Egyptian sign for 'life' (*ānkh*). In addition to the helmet he wears a bead collar, a shrine-shaped pectoral suspended from the neck and a pleated kilt with an animal's tail at the back. His feet are bare. The god standing in front of him, Amon-Re, holds with one hand the sign for 'life' to the king's nostrils and places the other hand on the king's shoulder.

This trumpet was found in a long chest in the Antechamber. It may have been taken there by the robbers from the Burial Chamber. The silver trumpet, wrapped in a reed cover, was left in the south-east corner of the chamber outside the outermost golden shrine.

Length 49.4 cm, maximum diameter 9.5 cm, minimum diameter 1.8 cm.

Carter II: 19 pl IIB; Desroches-Noblecourt 66; Hickman 17–19; Paris Exh no 39.

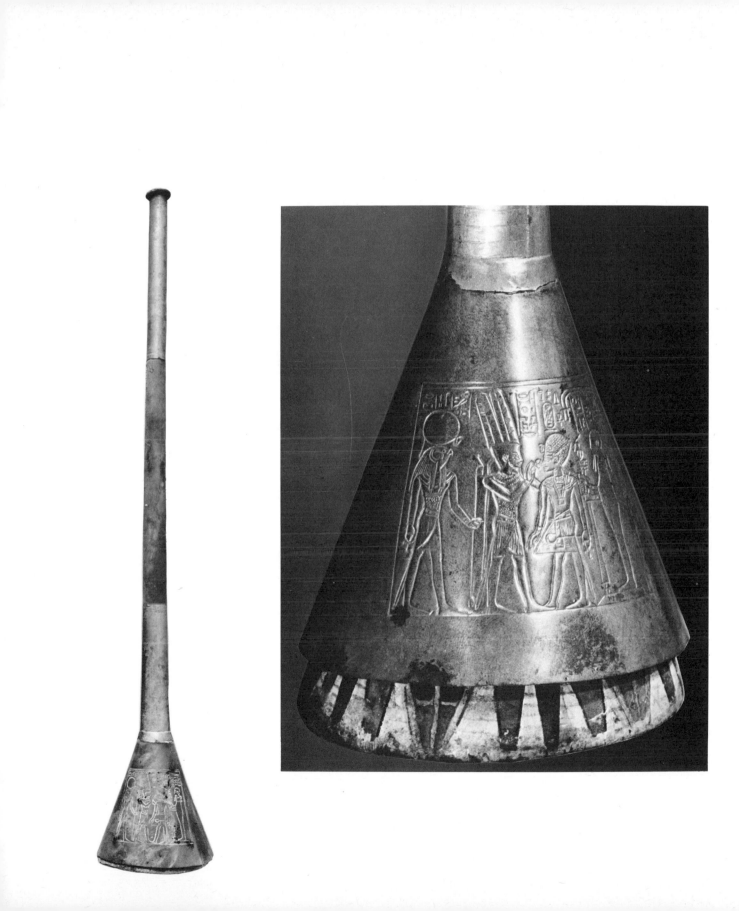

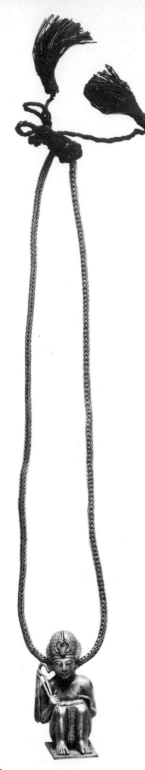

This figure of solid gold was found, wrapped in a piece of linen, within the gilded miniature coffin displayed in this exhibition (no 47). It represents a king wearing the *khepresh* crown (see no 22) with uraeus and a kilt with the regular apron in front. The upper part of his body, apart from a bead necklace, and his arms and legs below the knee are bare. In his right hand he holds the crook and flail (see no 44); the left hand rests on his knee. At the back of the neck is a loop for the plaited gold suspension chain. Instead of a clasp, linen cords terminating in tassels are attached to the upper ends of the chain for fastening the necklace.

In addition to this figure, the gilded coffin contained two smaller coffins, one inside the other, the innermost being inscribed with the name of Amenophis III's wife, Queen Tiy, and preserving a lock of her auburn hair. It has therefore been conjectured that the squatting figure represents Amenophis III (c 1417–1379 BC), but in the absence of an inscription the identity cannot be proved. Howard Carter regarded the figure and the lock of hair as heirlooms which were buried with Tutankhamun because he was the last successor of Amenophis III in the direct line of descent. Other writers have considered them as evidence that Amenophis III and Tiy were the parents of Tutankhamun (see above, p 12). Both the gilded coffin and the outermost wooden coffin, however, bore the names of Tutankhamun, and it seems more probable that the figure represents this king himself. In support of this identification is the fact

that the lobes of the ears are pierced for earrings, a feature seldom shown in representations of kings before Akhenaten (see no 39).

Egyptian kings and nobles are often shown on monuments wearing necklaces with pendants, and a number of the finest pieces of this kind from the tomb of Tutankhamun are included in this exhibition. As a rule, however, such pendants were amuletic in character, or at least reproduced mythological events. A squatting king is both exceptional iconographically and difficult to understand in its underlying conception. The pose is at first sight suggestive of the representations of the sun-god as a child squatting on a lotus flower, who is also sometimes depicted holding the crook and flail in one hand. The lotus flower was, however, an essential element in the composition of the scene because it provided the support for the sun-god when he emerged from Nun, the primordial waters, to bring light to the universe at the time of its creation. In this pendant the king is squatting on a thin plate of gold and, although he is young in appearance, he is clearly not a child. In Egyptian art kings, unless they were engaged in some recognizable activity such as hunting, warfare or religious ceremonies, were usually portrayed either standing or seated on a throne. Even before the end of the reign of Amenophis III, however, conventional styles were undergoing changes, which developed rapidly under Akhenaten and continued, in a more restrained form, under Tutankhamun. It is therefore not improbable that the figure, whether it represents Amenophis III or Tutankhamun, is merely an example of the many artistic innovations of the time which possessed no symbolical significance and were soon discarded.

▷ Colour

Height 5.4 cm.
Length of chain 54.0 cm,
Depth of chain 0.3 cm.

Carter III: 86–7, pl XXVc; Desroches-Noblecourt 134–5, pl IIIa.

Miniature coffin of wood overlaid with gesso and gilded with a feather pattern decoration. In style it is royal, except that it lacks the usual emblems on the brow, the uraeus and the head of a vulture. Also missing are the Osirian crook and flail, for which holes are provided (one covered with gold) in the hands. The arms and the upper part of the body are enveloped in the wings of vultures, symbolizing either Nekhbet and Wadjet or perhaps Isis and Nephthys. Beneath the talons, which grasp the sign for 'eternity' (*shen*), is engraved a magical spell, the end of which is blurred: 'Words spoken by the Osiris, the King Nebkheperure, deceased, "O my mother, Nut, spread thyself over me, that thou mayest place me among the Imperishable Stars which are in thee and I die not again"'. Under the feet is a figure of Isis with arms outstretched. The accompanying spell reads: 'Words spoken by Isis, "I have come that I may protect thee, O Osiris; thou shalt not be weary, these thy limbs shall not be tired, O Osiris"'.

This coffin is the second of four coffins diminishing in size, placed one inside another. It has adhered to the outermost coffin owing to the resin with which the inside of the latter was coated, and no method of separation has yet been found. On the outside of the smallest coffin, which is only 12.5 centimetres in length, are engraved the titles and the name of Queen Tiy, wife of Amenophis III (*c* 1417–1379 BC) and within it was found a plaited lock of her auburn hair. The uninscribed statuette of a king (no 46) lay between the second and the third coffins. If the statuette

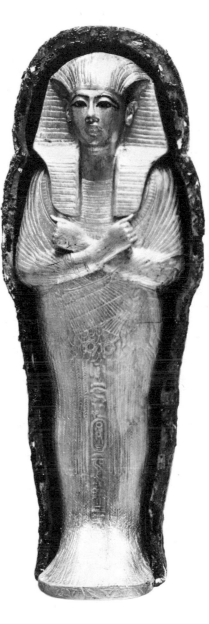

could be shown to represent Amenophis III, its presence in the tomb with the lock of Tiy's hair would lend support to the theory that Tiy and Amenophis were Tutankhamun's parents, as some authorities have supposed (see p 12). Ushabti figures were often placed in model coffins, but this is the only known example of such a coffin with contents of this kind. It was found in the Treasury, placed on top of the wooden shrine-shaped boxes which contained Ushabti figures.

Length 76.0 cm, maximum width 26.5 cm.

Carter III: 86–7, pl XXVA; Desroches-Noblecourt 135.

The shape of this ivory piece shows that it was intended to represent a boomerang (or throw-stick), in spite of the unsuitability of the material for practical use. Capped with gold and inscribed with the prenomen of the king, 'Beloved of (the god) Ptah, south of his wall', it is clearly a model, perhaps made for ritualistic purposes. Unlike actual boomerangs, one end is shaped like the handle of an axe or a hoe. The objects in the tomb included several wooden boomerangs which could have been used by the king in his life.

Fowling in the swamps of the Nile was a sport practised by the Egyptian nobles from early times. As a desirable occupation in the Next World it was represented on the walls of their tombs, the deceased owner being shown in the act of throwing his boomerang at birds rising from the swamp. One of the finest illustrations of the scene is in the Egyptian collection of this Museum. It shows a high official, who lived about a hundred years earlier than King Tutankhamun, standing in a boat made of papyrus stems, accompanied by his wife and daughter. In one hand he holds three live birds and in the other a serpent-boomerang. His tame goose stands in the prow of the boat and his cat leaps at a bird. It is uncertain whether the cat is retrieving a bird which has been stunned by a blow from Nebamun's boomerang or making its own capture, the purpose of the cat in the latter case being to disturb the birds so that they would rise above the papyrus flowers, thereby enabling the fowler to throw his boomerang at them without obstruction.

Among the magical spells written on the sides of the wooden coffins of nobles, five hundred years before the time of Tutankhamun, is an assurance to the deceased that the wadis of the Next World will be full of water, so that he may 'pluck papyrus flowers and marsh flowers, lotus and lotus buds. Waterfowl will rise by the thousand as (he) passes by. When (he) directs his boomerang against them a thousand will fall through the rush of air, geese, duck and many other kinds of fowl'. Both the wording of this spell and the painted representations on the walls of tombs would suggest that the deceased person was concerned only with providing himself with magical means for ensuring a continuance of his earthly pleasures and supplies of food in the Next World, but it is also possible that, by the time of Tutankhamun, the scene had acquired a symbolical significance without, however, necessarily excluding its original purpose. If the latter be true, the birds would represent marsh-dwelling demons of the Next World, who were a menace to the safety of the tomb-owner in the Afterlife.

The boomerang was found in the Annexe, placed in a wooden box with several wooden boomerangs.

Length 50.0 cm, width 3.5 cm, thickness 0.8 cm.

Carter III: pl XXXI; Desroches-Noblecourt 270; Paris Exh no 38.

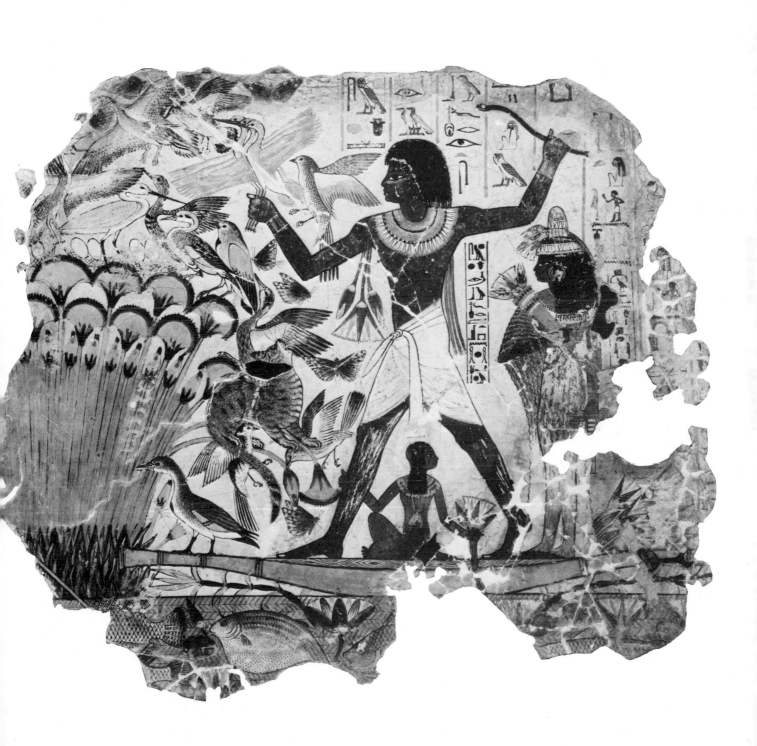

In the intricacy of its decoration this angular bow is one of the most elaborate of some fifty weapons of its class found in the tomb of Tutankhamun. It is composed of a thin wooden stave overlaid on both faces with a middle layer of a gelatinous substance (perhaps decayed sinew) which has been moulded on the inner face to form a keel, and an outer layer of tree-bark (possibly birch). Both the 'back' and the 'face' are ornamented symmetrically on each side of the grip with geometric, chevron and floral motifs inlaid and bordered with gold, gold granulations and gold bands. The pattern is broken on the 'face' by clumps of papyrus in flower and on the 'back' by figures of an ibex and a horse. Both animals are represented in association with flowers, which are difficult to identify. Perhaps the flowers with the ibex – a desert animal – are some species of desert plant, while the two clumps shown beneath the horse may be lotus. Ostrich plumes adorn the horse's headstall and an ostrich-plume fan is shown behind its flank (see no 23).

This bow was found in the Ante-chamber enclosed in a wooden box containing articles of clothing, sticks and arrows, the mixture probably being the result of the robbers' activities. As a weapon, the simple bow was used by the Egyptians in predynastic times and throughout their history, but the composite bow, of which this is an example, was not introduced until about three centuries before the time of Tutankhamun, when it was brought to Egypt by immigrants from Asia, known as the Hyksos. With it they also brought the horse-drawn chariot and it was probably the possession of these two advanced weapons which first enabled them to subjugate the Egyptian people. By gumming a sinew to a simple bow, the elasticity of the stave was greatly increased and its range was thereby considerably extended.

Length 1.03 m, width 2.3 cm, thickness 1.0 cm.

Carter 1: 114; McLeod 25 (no 27). Paris Exh no 22.

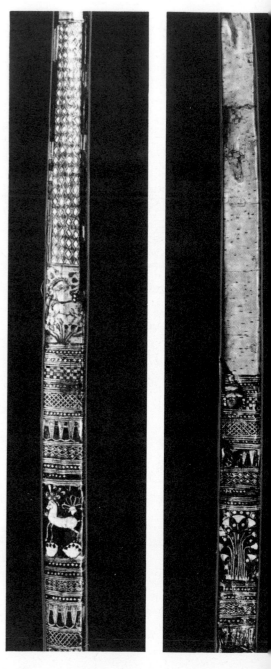

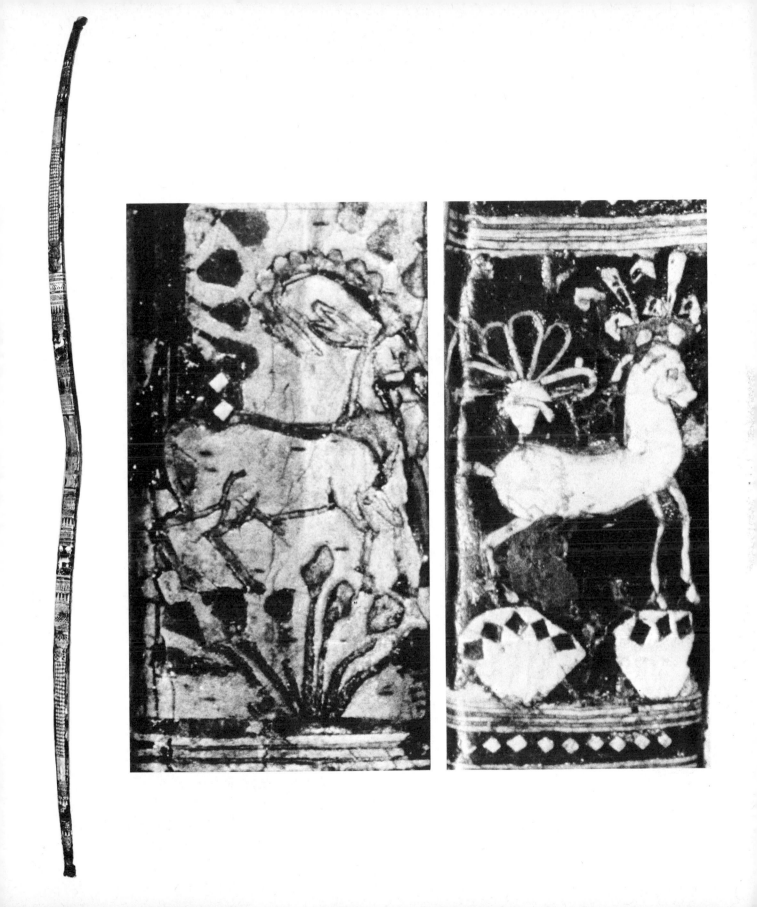

▷ Colour

This mask of solid gold, beaten and burnished, was placed over the head and shoulders of Tutankhamun's mummy, outside the linen bandages in which the whole body was wrapped. The stripes of the *nemes* headdress are made of blue glass in imitation of lapis lazuli, and the same material has been used for the inlay of the plaited false beard. The vulture's head upon the brow, symbolizing sovereignty over Upper Egypt, is also made of solid gold, apart from the beak, which is of horn-coloured glass, and the inlay of the eyes which is missing. By its side is the cobra, symbolizing sovereignty over Lower Egypt, its body made of solid gold, its head of dark blue faience, its eyes of gold cloisonné inlaid with translucent quartz backed with a red pigment, and its hood inlaid with carnelian, lapis lazuli, turquoise-coloured glass and quartz. The eyebrows, eyelids and kohl-marks extending sideways from the eyes are made of lapis lazuli and the eyes of quartz and obsidian. Caruncles are shown on the inner and outer canthi of the eyes (see no 1). The lobes of the ears are pierced for earrings, but when the mask was found the holes were covered with disks of gold foil. A triple-string necklace of gold and faience disk-beads has also been removed from the mask in order to reveal the neck. On the chest extending from shoulder to shoulder is a broad collar encrusted with segments of lapis lazuli, quartz and green felspar with a lotus-bud border of coloured glass cloisonné work. At each end of the collar is a terminal in the form of a falcon's head of gold encrusted with obsidian and coloured glass.

Mummification and the various rites connected with it had a double purpose: the preservation of the body to receive the soul and the creation of a likeness of the god Osiris. Through the action of imitative magic a dead body, mummified and bandaged so that outwardly it resembled the form of Osiris, would, so the Egyptians believed, be reanimated in the same way as the body of the god had been revivified after death, thereby enabling him to become ruler of the kingdom of the dead. Tutankhamun's body was mummified and bandaged in the prescribed Osirian fashion, and a crook and flail, the emblems of Osiris (see no 44), were placed in artificial hands of burnished gold outside the bandages over his chest. A hieroglyphic inscription on a strip of gold beneath the hands puts the following words in the mouth of the sky-goddess Nut: 'O Osiris, King of Upper and Lower Egypt and Lord of the Two Lands Nebkheperure, thy soul liveth and thy veins are healthy'. It is clear therefore that the dead king was regarded as an Osiris. But the Osirian creed never superseded completely the solar cult of the Pyramid Age, according to which deceased kings were thought to become identified with the sun-god Re, whose body was made of gold and his hair of lapis lazuli. Tutankhamun's mask with its gold face and neck, and its eyebrows and eyelashes of lapis lazuli, perhaps preserves a relic of this belief. The hands, which are the only other physical members represented, being also of gold, help to create the illusion that the whole body was made of this metal, an illusion which is heightened by the darkening effect of the unguents which had been applied to all the linen bandages.

The inscription engraved on the shoulders and on the back of the mask is a spell which first appears on masks of the Middle Kingdom, some five hundred years before the time of Tutankhamun. It was later incorporated in the Book of the

Dead (chapter 151B). Intended for the protection of the mask, it identifies its various parts with the corresponding physical members of different gods, addressing them individually: '... Thy right eye is the night bark (of the sun-god), thy left eye is the day-bark, thy eyebrows are (those of) the Ennead of the Gods, thy forehead is (that of) Anubis, the nape of thy neck is (that of) Horus, thy locks of hair are (those of) Ptah-Sokar. (Thou art) in front of the Osiris (Tutankhamun), he sees thanks to thee, thou guidest him to the goodly ways, thou smitest for him the confederates of Seth so that he may overthrow thine enemies before the Ennead of the Gods in the great Castle of the Prince, which is in Heliopolis ... the Osiris, the King of Upper Egypt Nebkheperure, deceased, given life by Re'.

Although it is difficult to judge how closely the face represents a true likeness of the king, it is at least an approximation. The rather narrow eyes, the shape of the nose, the fleshy lips and the cast of the chin are all in agreement with the features visible in his mummy, and the whole countenance is unmistakably youthful. Perhaps it is slightly idealized, but essentially it seems to be a faithful portrait.

Height 54.0 cm, width 39.0 cm, depth 49.0 cm.

Carter II: 83, 85, 88, frontispiece, pls XXV, LXXIII; Desroches-Noblecourt 74, 236, 300, fig 73, pl XXVI; Aldred 88, pl 158; Drioton 42; Fox pls 32, 33; Lange and Hirmer 467–8, pl XXXVIII; Piankoff pl 17; Paris Exh no 43; Japan Exh no 45.

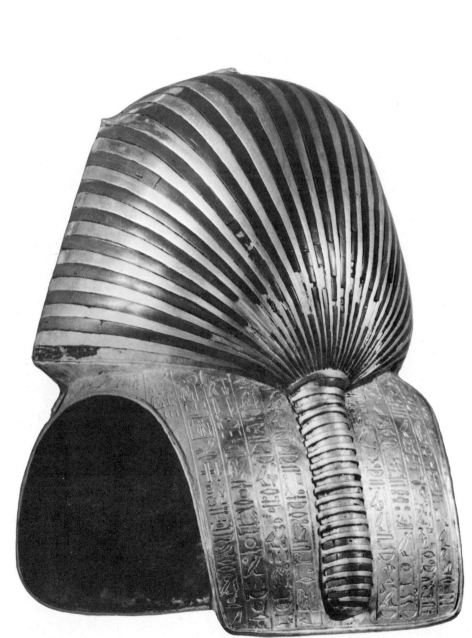

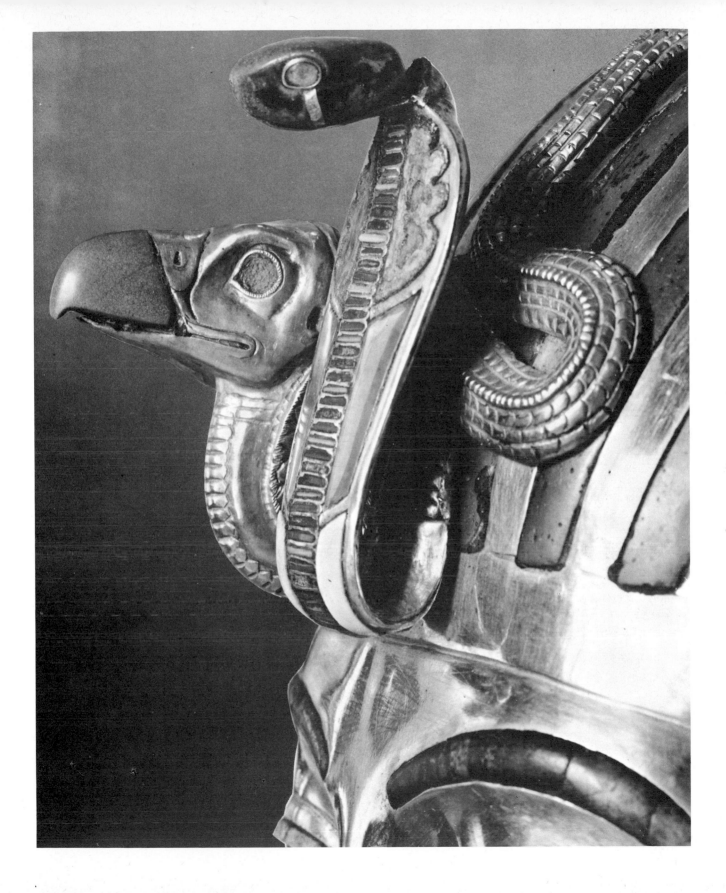

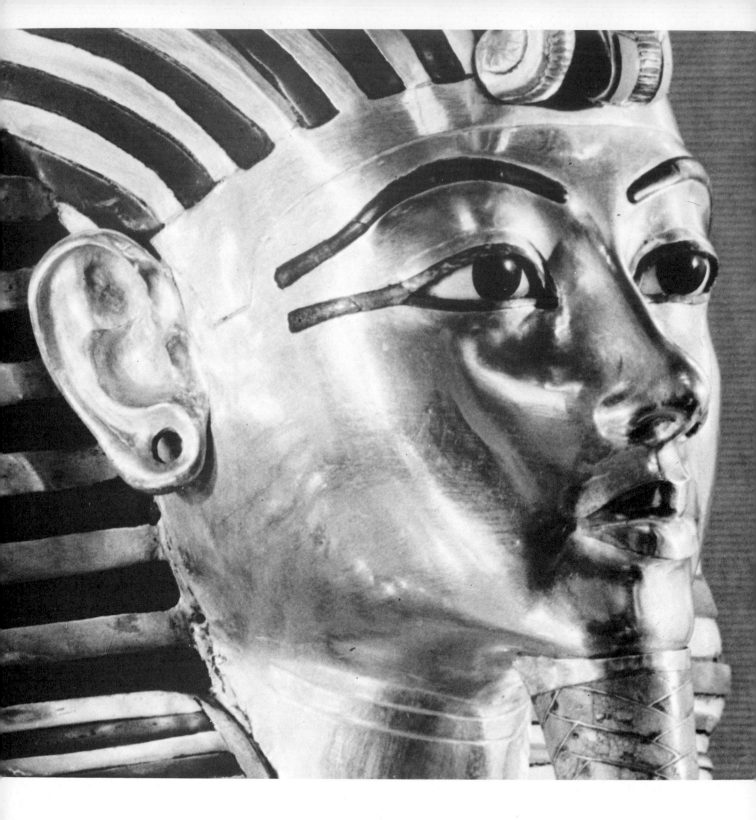

# KEY TO BIBLIOGRAPHICAL REFERENCES

ALDRED, C. *New Kingdom Art in Ancient Egypt* (2nd edition). London 1961.

BAKER, H. S. *Furniture in the Ancient World, Origins and Evolution, 3000–476 BC.* London 1966.

BONNET, H. *Reallexikon der ägyptischen Religionsgeschichte.* Berlin 1952.

CARTER, H. *The Tomb of Tut·Ankh·Amen.* Three vols. (Vol I with A. C. Mace.) London 1923–33.

ČERNÝ, J. *Hieratic Inscriptions from the Tomb of Tut'ankhamun* (*Tut'ankhamun's Tomb* Series II). Oxford 1965.

DESROCHES-NOBLECOURT, C. *Tutankhamen, Life and Death of a Pharaoh.* London 1963.

DRIOTON, E. *Le Musée du Caire* (*Encyclopédie photographique de l'art.* Ed Tel). Paris 1949.

FAIRMAN, H. W. 'The Myth of Horus at Edfu', *Journal of Egyptian Archaeology*, vol 21 (1935), 26–36.

FOX, P. *Tutankhamun's Treasure.* London 1951.

GARDINER, A. H. 'Tut'ankhamun's Gold Dagger', *Journal of Egyptian Archaeology*, vol 27 (1941), I (frontispiece).

HICKMAN, H. *La trompette dans l'Égypte ancienne* (*Supplément aux Annales du Service des Antiquités de l'Égypte*, Cahier no I). Cairo 1946.

KEIMER, L. 'Egyptian Formal Bouquets (Bouquets Montés).' *American Journal of Semitic Languages and Literatures*, vol XLI (1925), 145–161.

LANGE, K. and HIRMER, M. *Egypt – Architecture, Sculpture, Painting in three thousand years.* London 1968.

LUCAS, A. *Ancient Egyptian Materials and Industries* (4th edition, revised and enlarged by J. R. Harris). London 1962.

LYTHGOE, A. M. 'Excavations at the South Pyramid of Lisht in 1914'. *Ancient Egypt*, 1915, 147–53.

MCLEOD, W. *Composite Bows from the Tomb of Tut'ankhamun* (*Tut'ankhamun's Tomb* Series III). Oxford 1970.

MÖLLER, G. *Die Metallkunst der alten Ägypter.* Berlin 1924.

NEEDLER, W. 'A Thirty-square Draught Board in the Royal Ontario Museum.' *Journal of Egyptian Archaeology*, Vol 39 (1953), 60–75.

NEWBERRY, P. E. 'The Shepherd's Crook and the so-called "Flail" or "Scourge" of Osiris.' *Journal of Egyptian Archaeology*, vol 15 (1929), 84–94.

NIMS, C. F. *Thebes of the Pharaohs.* London 1965.

PIANKOFF, A. *The Shrines of Tut-ankh-Amon.* Bollingen Series XL 2. New York 1955.

PIEPER, M. *Das Brettspiel der alten Ägypter und seine Bedeutung für den ägyptischen Totenkult.* Berlin 1909.

PIEPER, M. 'Ein Text über das ägyptische Brettspiel.' *Zeitschrift für ägyptische Sprache*, vol 66 (1931), 16–33.

QUIBELL, J. E. *Excavations at Saqqara* (1911–12), *The Tomb of Hesy.* Cairo 1913.

RIESTERER, P. P. *Egyptian Museum Cairo, The Funeral Treasure of Tutankhamen.* Zurich 1966.

SCHAEFFER, C. F.-A. *Ugaritica* II (*Mission de Ras Shamra*, Tome v). Paris 1949.

SCHULMAN, 'The Berlin "Trauerrelief" ' (no 12411) and Some Officials of Tut'ankhamūn and Ay.' *Journal of the American Research Center in Egypt*, vol IV (1965), 55–68.

SINGER, C., HOLMYARD, E. J. and HALL, A. R. *A History of Technology*, vol I, Ch 25 'Fine Wood-Work' by Cyril Aldred. Oxford 1955.

TAIT, G. A. D. 'The Egyptian Relief Chalice.' *Journal of Egyptian Archaeology* vol 49 (1963), 93–139.

VANDIER, J. *Manuel d'archéologie égyptienne*, vol III, *Les Grandes Époques : La Statuaire.* Tomes I et 2. Paris 1958.

VILÍMKOVÁ, M., ABDUL-RAHMAN, M. H. and DARBOIS, D. *Egyptian Jewellery.* London 1969.

WILKINSON, A. *Ancient Egyptian Jewellery.* London 1971.

YOYOTTE, J. *Treasures of the Pharaohs.* Geneva 1968.

ZABKAR, L. V. *A Study of the Ba Concept in Ancient Egyptian Texts.* Chicago 1968.

Photographs supplied as follows:

*Page* 1/GI: 4–5/GI: 6/GI: 24/photo L. F. Husson by permission of Princeton University Press: 25/GR: 26/Times: 28–29/MMA: 30, 31, 32/MMA, gift of Theodore M. Davies, 1909: 33/GI: 34–35/Times: 36/MMA: 37/GR: 38/Times: 39 (all three)/Times: 41/Times: 42, 43, 44, 45/GI: 46/Times: 47/GI.

*Colour* 1, 7, 8, 10, 12, 13, 15, 18, 20, 23, 25, 26, 27, 30, 33, 36, 43, 46, 50/GR, F. L. Kenett: 28/GR, John Ross: 35/T & H, Albert Shoucair.

*Exhibits* 1 (all three)/Rapho: 2 (left)/Rapho; (right)/Cen Doc: 3, 4 (all three)/Cen Doc: 5, 6/Cen Doc: 7, 8/GI: 9 (all five)/SI: 10 (two on left)/Cen Doc; (two on right)/Rapho: 11 (left)/CM; (centre)/GI; (right)/SI: 12 (drawing)/PJ; 12/GI: 13 (first and second pages)/Cen Doc; (third page)/CM: 14 (all five)/CM: 15/GI: 16 (first page, left)/CM; (first page, right)/GI; (second page, left)/CM; (second page, two on right)/GI: 17 (all four)/Cen Doc: 18/GI: 19, 20/Cen Doc: 21 (first page)/Cen Doc; (second page, top)/GI; (second page, drawing)/PJ; (third page)/Cen Doc; (fourth page, top)/GI; (fourth page, bottom)/Cen Doc: 22 (first page)/SI; (second page, left)/SI; (second page, right)/CM: 23 (first page, left and right)/Cen Doc; (second page, drawings)/PJ: 24/GI: 25 (drawing)/PJ; 25 (all seven)/Cen Doc: 26, 27/GI: 28/GR, John Ross: 29, 30, 31/GI: 32 (both)/Cen Doc: 33/GI: 34 (both)/SI: 35/CM: 36 (drawing)/PJ; (first page and both on second page)/SI; (third page)/Rapho: 37 (both)/GI: 38 (both)/CM: 39 (both)/Cen Doc: 40, 41, 42/GI: 43 (both)/Cen Doc: 44 (all four)/Cen Doc: 45 (left) Cen Doc; (right)/Rapho: 46, 47/GI: 48 (left)/GI; (right)/BM: 49 (first page, both)/Cen Doc; (second page, left)/CM; (second page, centre and right)/Rapho: 50 (first and fifth pages)/Rapho; (third and fourth pages)/Cen Doc.

Key to abbreviations

| | |
|---|---|
| GI | Griffith Institute, Oxford |
| GR | George Rainbird Ltd |
| Times | The Times Picture Library |
| MMA | Metropolitan Museum of Art, New York |
| T & H | Thames and Hudson Ltd |
| Rapho | Agence Rapho, Paris |
| Cen Doc | Centre of Documentation, Cairo |
| SI | Smithsonian Institution, Washington |
| CM | Cairo Museum |
| PJ | Mrs P. Johnson |
| BM | British Museum, London |